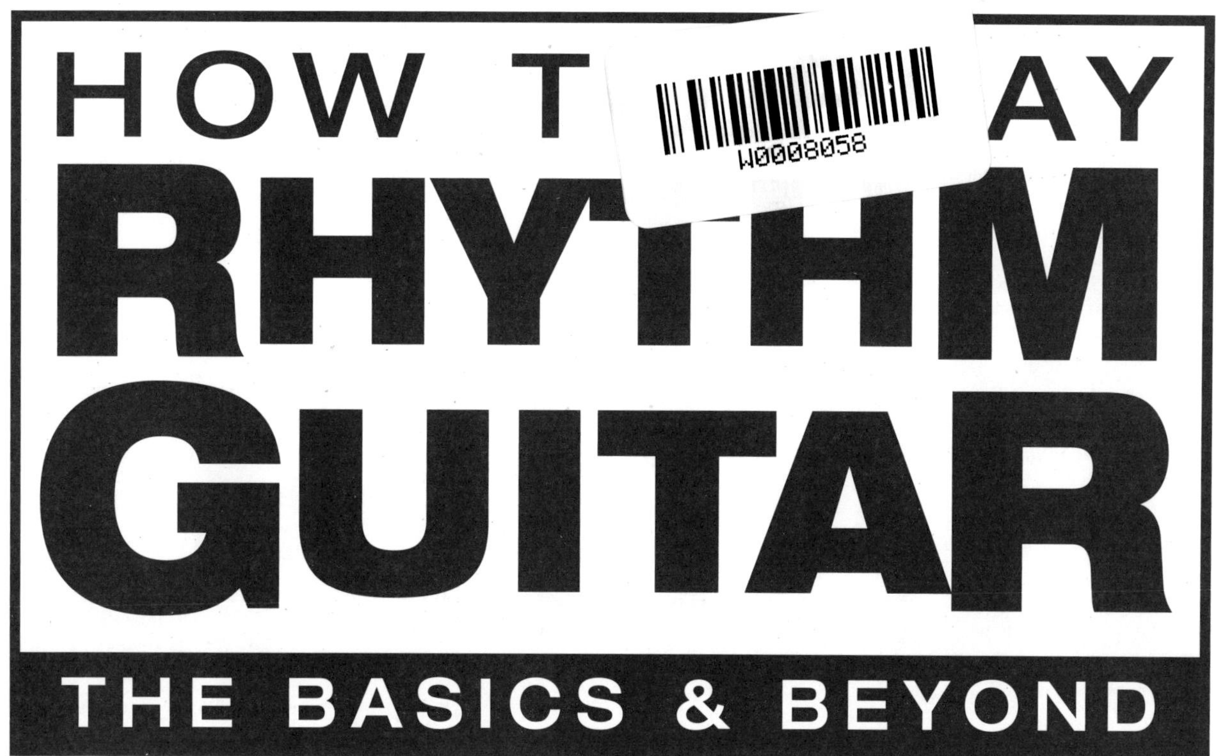

EDITED BY RICHARD JOHNSTON

San Francisco

Published by Backbeat Books
600 Harrison Street, San Francisco, CA 94107
www.backbeatbooks.com
email: books@musicplayer.com

An imprint of CMP Information, Inc.
Publishers of *Guitar Player, Bass Player, Keyboard,* and *EQ* magazines

Distributed to the book trade in the US and Canada by
Publishers Group West, 1700 Fourth Street, Berkeley, CA 94710

Distributed to the music trade in the US and Canada by
Hal Leonard Publishing, P.O. Box 13819, Milwaukee, WI 53213

Text and cover design by Richard Leeds — bigwigdesign.com
Cover photo by Ken Settle
Composition by Michael Baughan

Library of Congress Cataloging-in-Publication Data

How to play rhythm guitar : the basics & beyond / edited by Richard Johnston.
p. cm.
ISBN 0-87930-811-7 (alk. paper)
1. Guitar—Methods—Self-instruction. I. Johnston, Richard, 1947-

MT588.H67 2004
787.87'193—dc22

2004025008

Printed in the United States of America
04 05 06 07 08 5 4 3 2 1

CONTENTS

INTRODUCTION

It's about time. In Backbeat's How To Play series we've presented lessons on all-around 6-string knowledge, and we've explored essential styles such as rock, blues, and metal. While all of our How To Play books include information on chords and accompaniment, this is the first How To Play title devoted entirely to rhythm.

After all, while playing soulful blues lines and blazing rock solos will get you a certain self-indulgent satisfaction, it's the beat that moves the feet. As a well-rounded rhythm guitarist you'll join an elite group that can step into any situation and make the music hit listeners where it counts. And you'll be able to support those aspiring lead players—as well as singers and other soloists—in a way that will make you indispensable onstage or in a studio. In other words, we could call this book *How To Play Gigs on Guitar.*

So maybe you don't want to be a do-it-all player; you'd rather hone your rhythm skills in the music that moves you the most. Not a problem. *How To Play Rhythm Guitar* includes lessons by the top players and teachers in styles like blues, soul, rock, and reggae, and you'll learn the secrets of players like Keith Richards and Steve Cropper who have reached the rarified realms of the rhythm-guitar gods. All of these lessons come from the pages of *Guitar Player* magazine, which for nearly 40 years has been the single most authoritative voice of and for guitarists worldwide.

Words and printed music will take you a long way toward rhythmic righteousness, but eventually you have to engage your ears. That's why we've teamed with TrueFire.com to give you free online audio for all of the lessons in *How To Play Rhythm Guitar.* Check page 6.

For this installation of How To Play Guitar, thanks are due Backbeat production editor Amy Miller, music editor Jesse Gress, music engraver Liz Ledgerwood, and proofreader Karl Coryat, as well as Brad Wendkos, Alison Hasbach, and the rest of the TrueFire folks. And huge heaps of gratitude go to the writers, teachers, and players who keep the music grooving. Now it's your turn.

—Richard Johnston, Editor

ABOUT THE AUTHORS

Andy Bassford has performed with artists ranging from Toots & the Maytals and Ernest Ranglin to Bonnie Raitt and Trey Anastasio. In 2003 he received a JFM award for contributions to the Jamaican music industry.

Joe Deloro has arranged numerous guitar transciption books for Warner Bros. and Hal Leonard. His instructional articles have appeared in *Guitar Player, How To Play Guitar*, and *Acoustic Guitar* magazines. For more information, go to joedeloro.com.

Andy Ellis is a Senior Editor for *Guitar Player* magazine. An active performer, session player, and educator, Andy founded *Guitar Player*'s Sessions section and edited the book *Guitar Player Sessions* [Backbeat].

Joe Gore is a guitarist, producer, engineer, and arranger who has worked with artists such as Tom Waits, PJ Harvey, Bijou Phillips, the Eels, and Stella Soleil. Currently a *Guitar Player* contributing editor, he was a *GP* staff editor for more than ten years.

Jesse Gress is the author of Backbeat's *The Guitar Cookbook, Guitar Lick Factory*, and *Guitar Licks of the Brit-Rock Heroes*. A former *Guitar Player* music editor, Jesse tours and records with Todd Rundgren and the Tony Levin Band, and he has served as music editor on several Backbeat titles.

Adam Levy tours and records with Norah Jones and has also recorded with artists such as Leni Stern, Trevor Dunn, and Tracy Chapman. His own albums include *Buttermilk Channel* and *Get Your Glow On*, both on Lost Wax.

Dave Rubin, a.k.a. the "Blues Hound," is currently an author and freelance writer for the Hal Leonard Corporation, Truefire.com, and *Guitar One* magazine, and has been nominated for a 2004 W.C. Handy "Keepin' the Blues Alive" award. He resides in New York City where he gives private blues guitar lessons.

NOTATIONAL SYMBOLS

The following symbols are used in *How To Play Rhythm Guitar* to notate fingerings, techniques, and effects commonly used in guitar music. Certain symbols are found in either the tablature or the standard notation only, not both. For clarity, consult both systems.

4● : Left-hand fingering is designated by small Arabic numerals near note heads (1=first finger, 2=middle finger, 3=third finger, 4=little finger, t=thumb).

p● : Right-hand fingering designated by letters (p=thumb, i=first finger, m=middle finger, a=third finger, c=little finger).

②● : A circled number (1-6) indicates the string on which a note is to be played.

⊓ : Pick downstroke.

V : Pick upstroke.

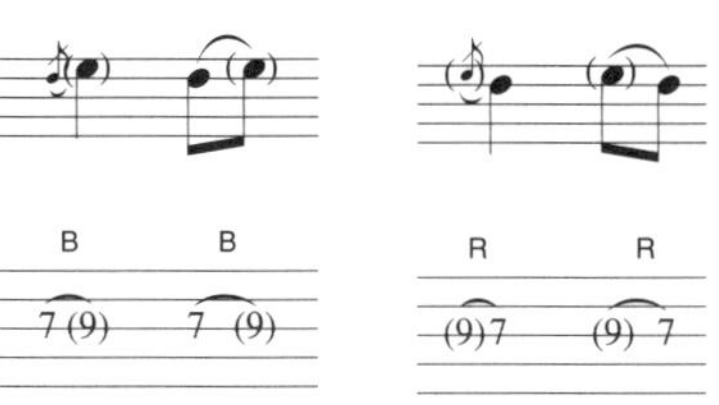

Bend: Play the first note and bend to the pitch of the equivalent fret position shown in parentheses.

Reverse Bend: Pre-bend the note to the specified pitch/fret position shown in parentheses. Play, then release to indicated pitch/fret.

Hammer-on: From lower to higher note(s). Individual notes may also be hammered.

Pull-off: From higher to lower note(s).

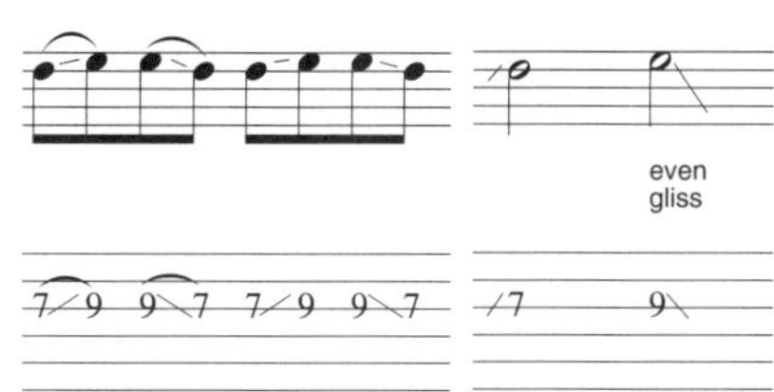

Slide: Play first note and slide up or down to the next pitch. If the notes are tied, pick only the first. If no tie is present, pick both.

A slide symbol before or after a single note indicates a slide to or from an undetermined pitch.

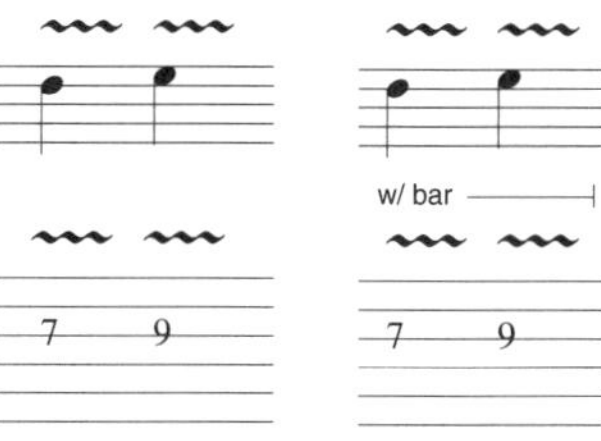

Finger vibrato. Bar vibrato.

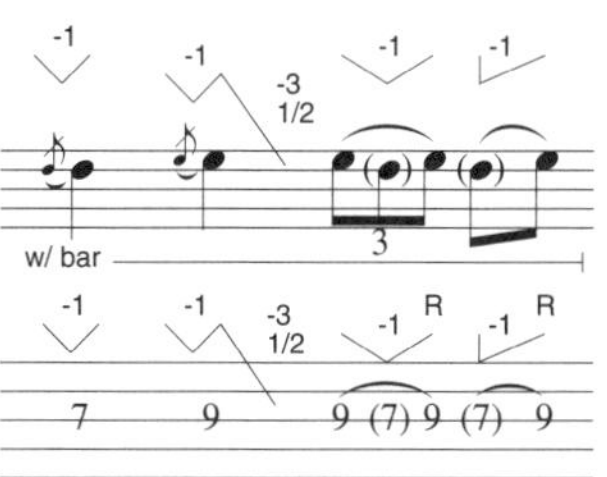

Bar dips, dives, and bends: Numerals and fractions indicate distance of bar bends in half-steps.

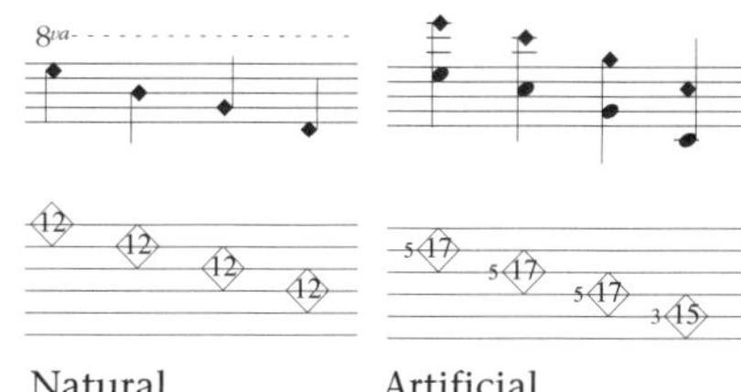

Natural harmonics. Artificial harmonics.

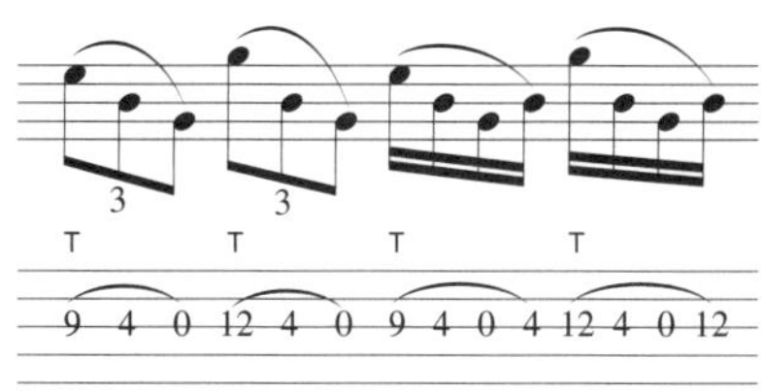

Pick-hand tapping: Notes are hammered with a pick-hand finger, usually followed by additional hammer-ons and pull-offs.

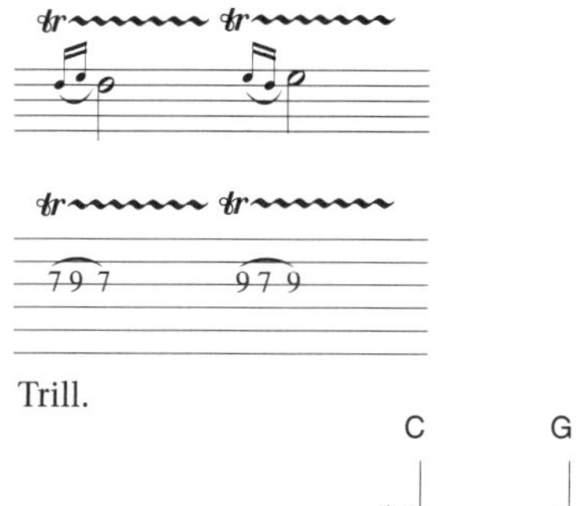

Trill.

C G

trem.

7 9

3 1 0 2 3 3 3 0 0 2 3

Tremolo picking.

Strum: Arrow heads indicate direction.

HOW TABLATURE WORKS

The horizontal lines represent the guitar's strings, the top line standing for the high *E*. The numbers designate the frets to be played. For instance, a 2 positioned on the first line would mean play the 2nd fret on the first string (0 indicates an open string). Time values are indicated on the standard notation staff seen directly above the tablature. Special symbols and instructions appear between the standard and tablature staves.

CHORD DIAGRAMS

In all chord diagrams, vertical lines represent the strings, and horizontal lines represent the frets. The following symbols are used:

▬ Nut; indicates first position.

X Muted string, or string not played.

○ Open string.

⌒ Barre (partial or full).

● Placement of left-hand fingers.

III Roman numerals indicate the fret at which a chord is located.

Arabic numerals indicate left-hand fingering.

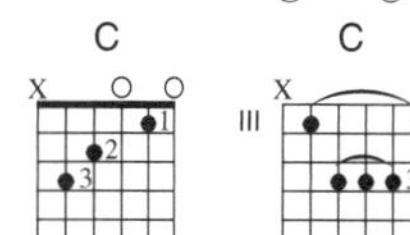

HOW TO PLAY RHYTHM GUITAR

FREE AUDIO LESSONS

All of the lessons featured in HOW TO PLAY RHYTHM GUITAR are available online, in audio MP3 format, for immediate download AT NO EXTRA COST. Now you can hear how the lesson examples are supposed to sound when played by the pros. Get your free audio lessons now and start learning the basics and beyond!

How to Get Your Earful

1) Go to PlayRhythm.TrueFire.com.
2) Register the Backbeat code printed on the inside back cover of this book.
3) Download lessons to your desktop.

$10 Bonus From TrueFire!

If you're new to TrueFire, after registering and downloading your lessons, you will be e-mailed a TrueFire Cash certificate good for $10 worth of additional lessons on TrueFire. Choose from over 1,200 killer guitar lessons written and performed by top artists and instructors.

A BRIEF HISTORY OF TIME

A Rhythm Guitar Primer

BY JESSE GRESS

Hey man, do you play rhythm or lead?" Pose this question to any classical guitarist and you're likely to find yourself on the receiving end of a quizzical stare or hysterical laughing fit.

Such distinctions—probably a byproduct of the early '60s surf instrumental craze—simply don't exist in the classical world. The majority of us, though (including those who despise the concept), live in an environment where the general public seems insistent upon segregating popular guitar playing into two camps: rhythm guitar, meaning chords, and lead guitar, referring to single-note soloing.

Before you scoff, consider this: They're not far off the mark, just a bit confused. These two aspects of guitar playing are more about *context* and *function* than style. "Rhythm guitar" actually translates to "accompaniment," while "lead guitar" describes the instrument as a featured melodic or solo voice. In reality, each "style" is cross-pollinated with elements of the other. Rhythm guitar parts typically incorporate diads (two-note chords) and repetitive single-note figures in addition to chords, while leads often blend chords or chordal fragments with single notes. Ultimately, both are defined by their context within a particular piece of music. Let's investigate the big picture.

The guitar gained popularity in this country as a cheap, portable source of accompaniment for rural folk, country, and spiritual singers before finding its way into the rhythm sections (a-ha!) of big bands and jazz combos and eventually becoming the cornerstone of rock 'n' roll. The following 25 musical examples—grouped by genre—present an abbreviated tour of the guitar's numerous rhythmic roles throughout the last century. Each includes picking and counting instructions between the staves. If you're unsure about note values and rhythmic division, spend some time with the sidebar and a metronome or drum machine. (You can also check out Backbeat's *The Guitar Cookbook* for a complete guide to rhythm, melody, and harmony.)

Traditional Folk & Country Styles

The earliest rhythm guitarists who played traditional folk songs could simply strum open chords to basic quarter-note rhythms while they crooned along. Example 1a shows a popular bass/chord variation on this basic strumming pattern. Finger the entire *Am7* chord, play its bass note—the open 5th string—and let it ring as you down-strum the rest of the chord for the remaining three beats of the measure. Repeat this measure and follow suit with the *D7*, *G7*, and *C* chords in bars 3 through 7. The single-note descending bass line in bar 8 provides a smooth and comfy transition back to the top of the progression.

Ex. 1a

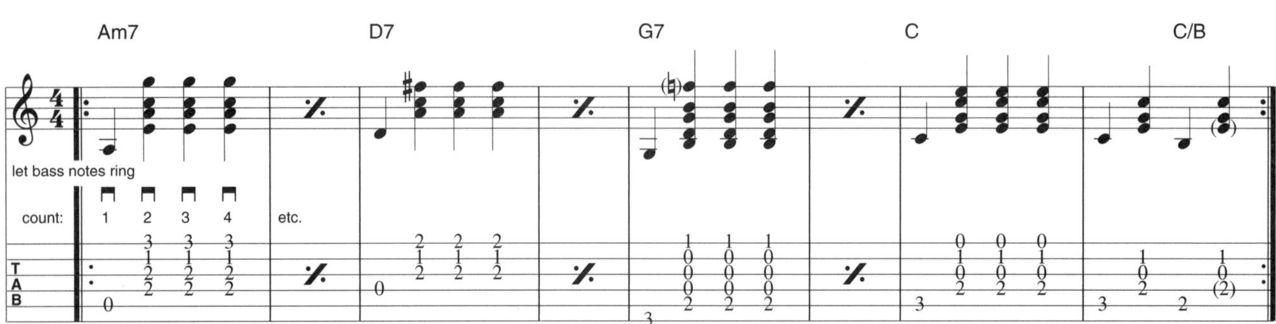

Another way to create a folky chordal backdrop is to arpeggiate chords and let each note ring. In Ex. 1b we take an arpeggiated approach to a popular folk progression by arranging the chords into six-note ascending/descending figures. Starting on its root, play each chord using three consecutive downstrokes followed by three upstrokes. The string skips in bars 1, 2, and 5 accommodate the root/bass notes while keeping a consistent picking pattern on the top three strings.

Ex. 1b

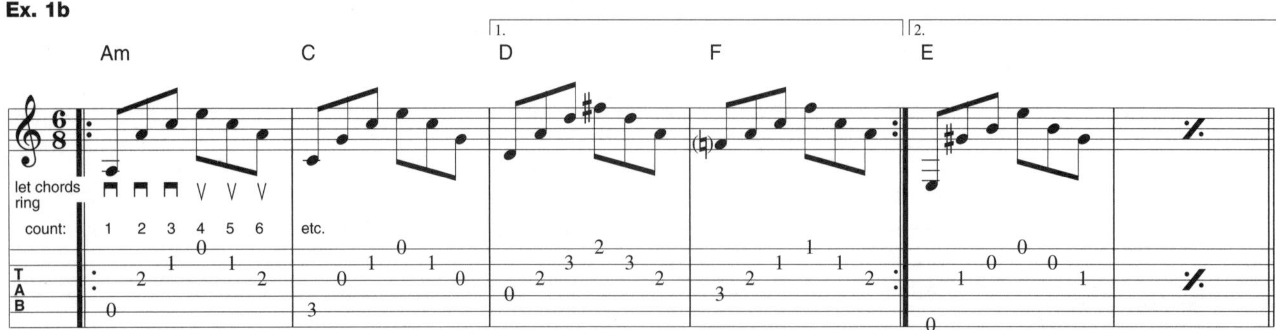

Traditional country pickers hotrodded the early folk accompaniment styles with faster tempos and busier single-note bass runs. Written in cut time (tap your foot on the half-notes), Ex. 2 borrows the opening *boom-chick* bass/chord technique from Ex. 1a but embellishes beat *three* of bars 1, 2, 3, 4, 5, and 7 with hammered midrange chord tones. Single-note bass runs make up three-quarters of bar 6 and all of bar 8.

Ex. 2

Country music pioneer Merle Travis set the standard for fingerstyle rhythm guitar, so much so that this style of fingerpicking was named in his honor. Example 3a illustrates Travis picking using an open *D* chord. To suss this style, dissect the one-bar pattern into four discrete movements—one per beat. Master each beat by repeating it as many times as necessary before adding the next and playing them in succession. Allow all of the notes to ring; soon, a smooth, flowing pattern will begin to emerge. Example 3b is a hybrid pick-and-fingers version of Travis-style picking applied to *D7*. Either technique can be easily adapted to any chord and tempo.

Ex. 3a **Ex. 3b**

Jazz Styles

When dixieland evolved into jazz, the archtop acoustic guitar was welcomed into the popular orchestras, big bands, and combos of the day, but its limited projection restricted guitarists to four-on-the-floor chordal comping within the rhythm section. It wasn't until the advent of the first amplified guitar that the instrument became an audible solo, or lead, voice. Prior to that, the idea—personified by Count Basie guitarist Freddie Green—was to create movement within a static chord by coloring it with extensions such as the 6 and 7, and by adding passing chords between these colorations.

Examples 4a–4c show how you can start embellishing the three basic chord sounds—major, minor, and dominant—with extensions and passing chords. Practice these moves in all keys, and experiment with any additional voicings you may know. Using this technique, you can transform the basic II–V–I–VI progression in Ex. 5a into the more propulsive rhythm figure in Ex. 5b.

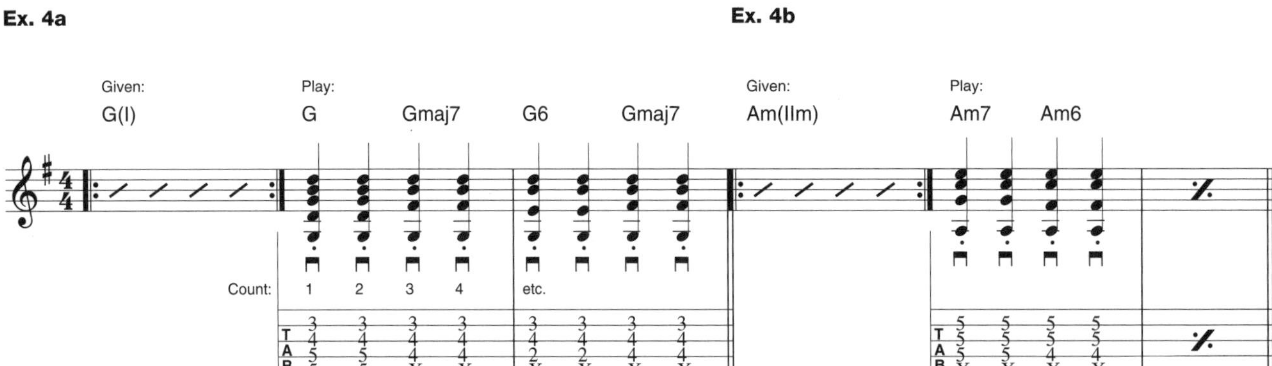

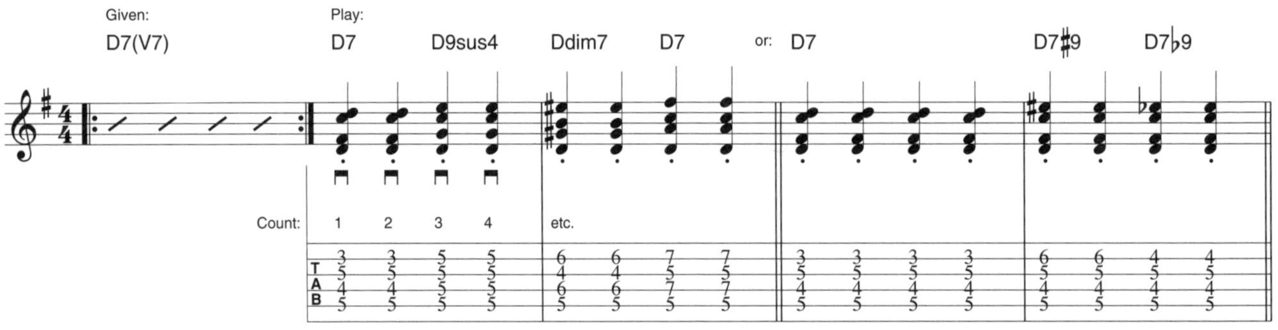

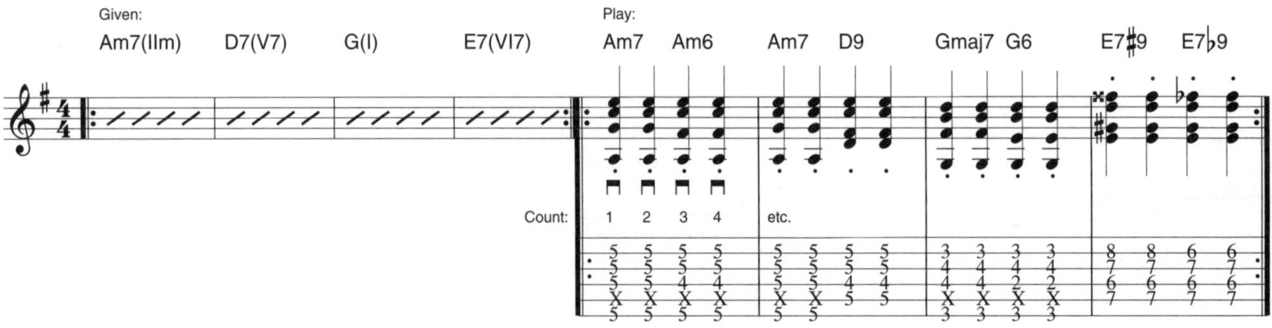

Example 6a illustrates an eight-bar excerpt from one of the most enduring progressions in jazz. Play it twice to form the entire 16-bar A-section. These "Rhythm" changes—named for the standard "I've Got Rhythm" (double a-ha!)—incorporate colorations and passing chords, and they fly by quickly at a rate of two per bar. Once you master the changes, try hitting only the bass note on the first beat of each chord. Though this is the same technique used for folk- and country-flavored *boom-chick* picking, these harmonically sophisticated chords create a whole different vibe.

Example 6b outlines the eight-bar bridge—four dominant-7th chords (*B7–E7–A7–D7*) that back-cycle through the circle of 5ths to form a III–VI–II–V progression. You can liven these up by transposing the dominant-7th embellishments from the first half of Ex. 4c to each chord change. Play Ex. 6a twice, Ex. 6b once, and Ex. 6a once more to complete the entire song form. (Bonus: Hum, sing, or whistle the themes from *The Flintstones* and *Leave It to Beaver* over the 32-bar progression.)

Ex. 6a

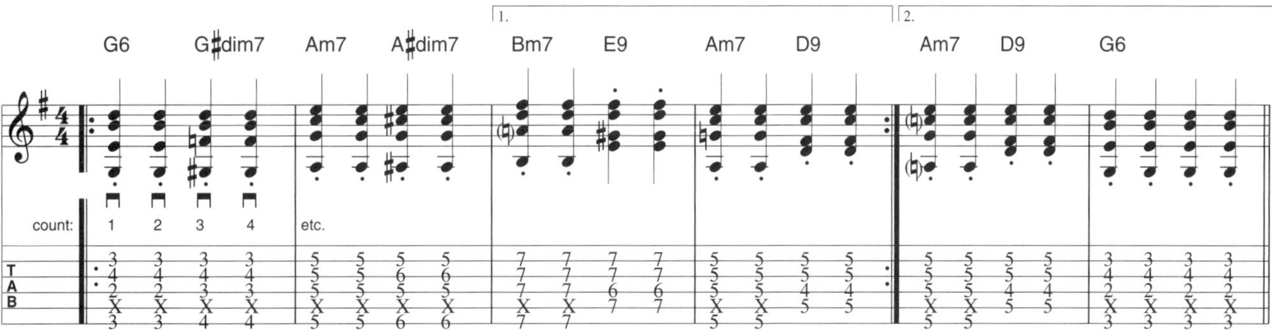

Ex. 6b

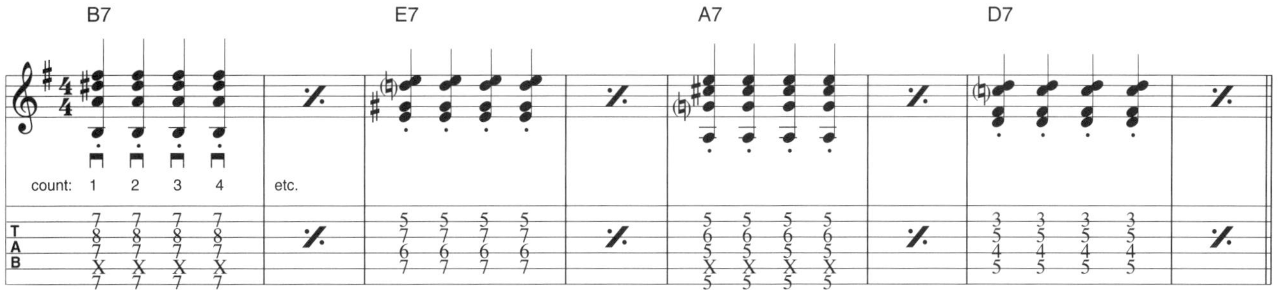

Blues Styles

As folk, country, and spirituals melded into the rural acoustic blues styles of the Mississippi and Louisiana deltas, their straightforward accompaniment became decorated with more intricate, vocal-like techniques, often played with a bottleneck slide and/or in open tunings. Example 7 keeps it simple with a country blues turnaround played over the last four bars of a standard 12-bar blues progression in *E*. The blend of chords and single bass notes is reminiscent of folk and country styles, but the slow shuffle rhythm and exclusive use of dominant-7th chords is all blues. The V-chord change utilizes an open *B7* voicing and single-note passing tones into the IV chord (*A7*), and bar 2 features two different *A7* voicings surrounding a barred *A6*. The *G–G#* bass run anticipates the actual turnaround in bars 3 and 4, which is played over bars 11 and 12 of the 12-bar blues form. Here, we pedal the open 1st and 2nd strings while the bass notes take a chromatic walk from the ♭7 (*D*) down to the 5 (*B*). Try breaking each beat in bar 3 into a bass/open-strings/bass pattern, or arpeggiate all three notes in ascending order—it's all good.

Ex. 7

The sophisticated, electric urban blues style spawned in Chicago—which would become highly influential to a future wave of British blues aficionados—is characterized by an "uptown" swing-eighth feel. Subsequently adopted by Texas blues men, the Chicago-style rhythm figures in Ex. 8a and Ex. 8b take different but complementary approaches to the same groove. The sliding and staccato 6th- and 9th-chord punctuations in Ex. 8a nail the downbeat and the "and" of beat *two*, while Ex. 8b features a single-note swing-eighth figure that doubles a typical bass line. Get the help of a friend or a recording device to hear both parts at the same time.

Ex. 8a

Ex. 8b

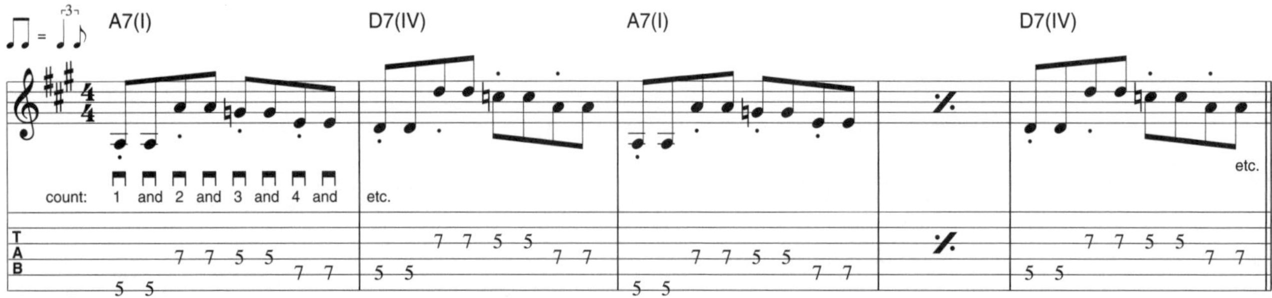

Early Rock 'n' Roll

Some say the blues had a baby and they called it rock 'n' roll, but it takes at least two to tango. Early rock 'n' roll—played on amplified electric guitars from its inception—was a generational cross-pollination of not only country and blues elements, but swing and Latin rhythms as well. For instance, forefather Chuck Berry borrowed rhythms and phrasing equally from country, big band, and blues styles, incorporating all of them into his music. Ironically, he became best known for the straight-eighth, barrelhouse/boogie-woogie style spotlighted in Ex. 9.

Ex. 9

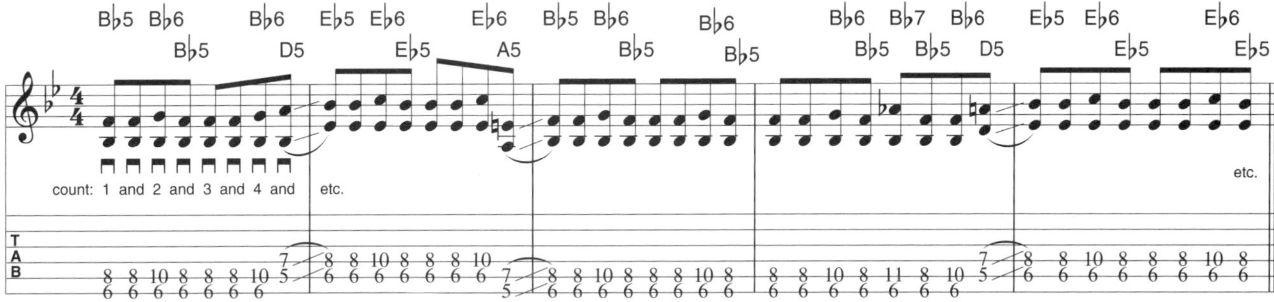

The infamous "Bo Diddley beat" depicted in Ex. 10—an adaptation of a long/short Latin clave rhythm—had already been modified and ingrained in American culture as "shave and a haircut, two bits" by the time Bo had made it famous in hits like "Hey! Bo Diddley." Mr. Diddley preferred his *F* chord with a capo at the 1st fret and a touch of amp tremolo.

Ex. 10

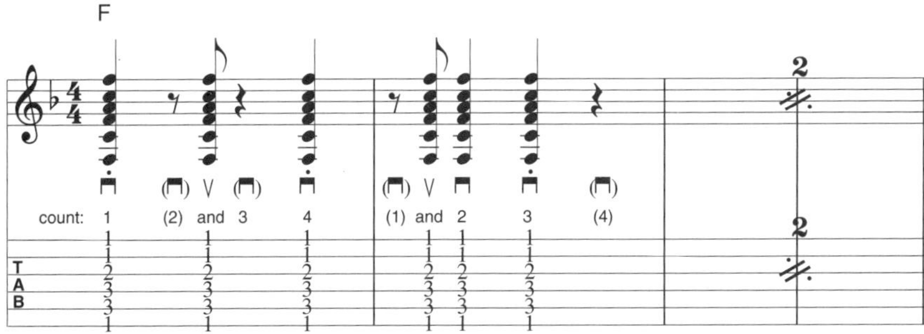

There has probably never been a clearer melding of country and blues than the Elvis Presley/Scotty Moore collaboration on the King's "Mystery Train." Moore made rockabilly history with moves like those in Examples 11a–11d, which adapt the alternating-bass fingerstyle made famous by Chet Atkins. Piece each example together the same way you learned Travis-style picking in Ex. 3a—one beat at a time. Example 11a utilizes an *E–E6* movement, while Ex. 11b reverses their order. Ex. 11c adds a hammered 3rd (*C♯*) and barred *A/E* fragment in place of *E6* and *E*. The last variation, Ex. 11d, is also the trickiest. The 3rd-less *E* chord on beat *two* is spread over four strings, and we hammer on a 6 while simultaneously thumbing the octave bass note on beat *four*. You can also play these examples with your pick and middle finger. When you're ready, you can transpose them up the fingerboard to *A* at the 5th fret and *B* at the 7th to play an entire 12-bar blues progression.

Ex. 11a Ex. 11b Ex. 11c Ex. 11d

Folk-Rock

By the time '60s rolled around, some acoustic guitarists had settled into an e-z folk-rock niche characterized by unspectacular but happy rhythms like those in Examples 12a–12c. Take them all at moderate tempos and note the similarity to many of the shoegazer rhythms prevalent in today's alternative rock music.

Ex. 12a Ex. 12b Ex. 12c

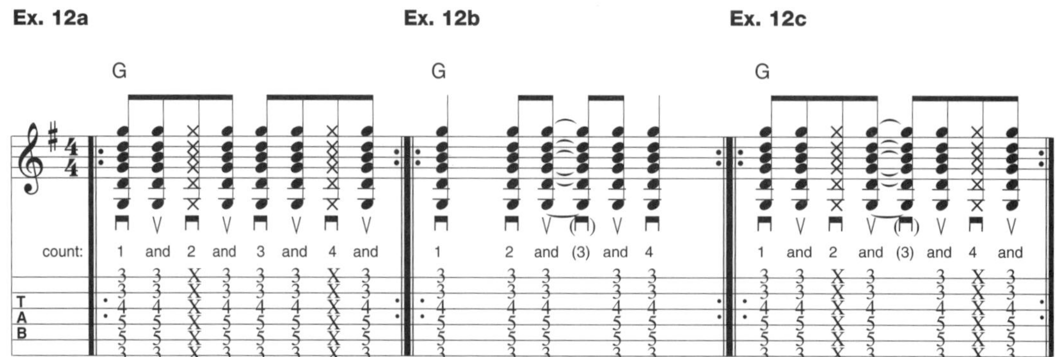

'60s & '70s Rock

Fortunately, the British invasion wasn't far behind. When the Beatles, the Rolling Stones, and the Who stormed our shores in the early '60s, they brought with them revolutionary new concepts in rhythm and lead guitar that reshaped rock music and remain vital to this day. Fueling their own skiffle roots with the energy of early American rock 'n' roll and R&B, this

Ex. 13a Ex. 13b

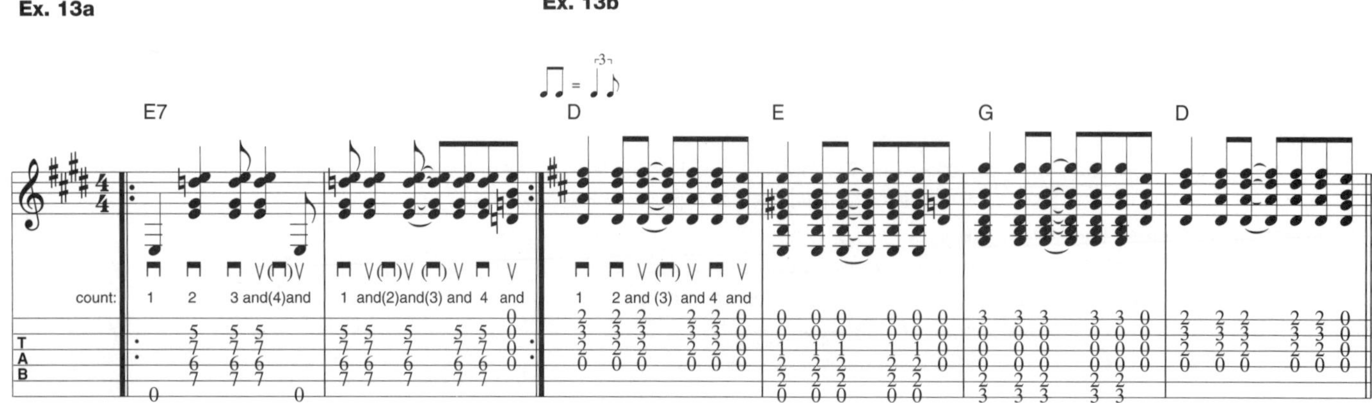

wave of bands laced their songs with rhythmic syncopation, or accented upbeats, and cranked their amps to previously unthinkable levels. And the kids loved it.

Example 13a motors along with a Beatle-y mix of straight and syncopated *E7* chords, utilizing the all-important, all-purpose passing chord on the "and" of beat *four* in bar 2. The basic rhythm in Ex. 13b looks folky, but its attitude and chord progression take it beyond that realm to someplace new and exciting.

The next two examples reveal the secret of Paul McCartney's "brushed" fingerstyle heard on Beatle songs such as "Yesterday" and "Blackbird." Examine the picking notation in Ex. 13c, which applies to the thumb and index finger, and you'll find a thumbed downstroke on the low-*E* root followed by a brushed up-down-up index finger motion on the top four strings. (Don't worry if you accidentally thumb or brush the 5th string; it's part of the *E* chord.) The rhythm figure in Ex. 13d is similarly made up of two identical halves, but this time we simultaneously brush the *G* chord on beat *one* (played on the inside four strings) in both directions—down with the thumb and up with the index finger—before completing the beat with a down-up index brush. The second beat completes the pattern with a thumbed downstroke on the *G* root followed by up-and-down index-finger brushes. Again, don't be concerned if the open 4th string occasionally sounds along with the thumbed roots—it's part of the *G* chord. Loop the one-bar figure until it flows smoothly.

Ex. 13c **Ex. 13d**

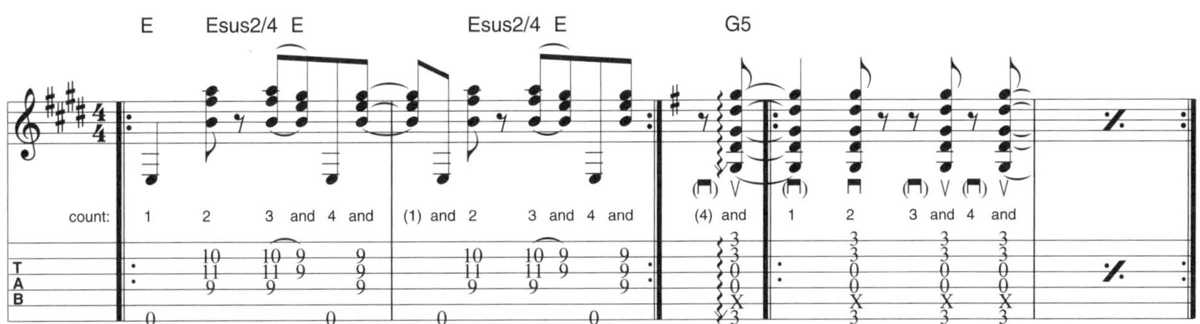

Grittier and harder rocking, the Rolling Stones were more affected by Chicago blues and American R&B than their Liverpool peers were. The rave-up rhythm riff in Ex. 14a lays down low open-*E* roots peppered with ninth-position *Esus2/sus4* pull-offs to tonic *E* triads. And while it's played with a country-rock feel, the syncopated one-chord rhythm figure in Ex. 14b borrows liberally from Howlin' Wolf and John Lee Hooker.

Ex. 14a **Ex. 14b**

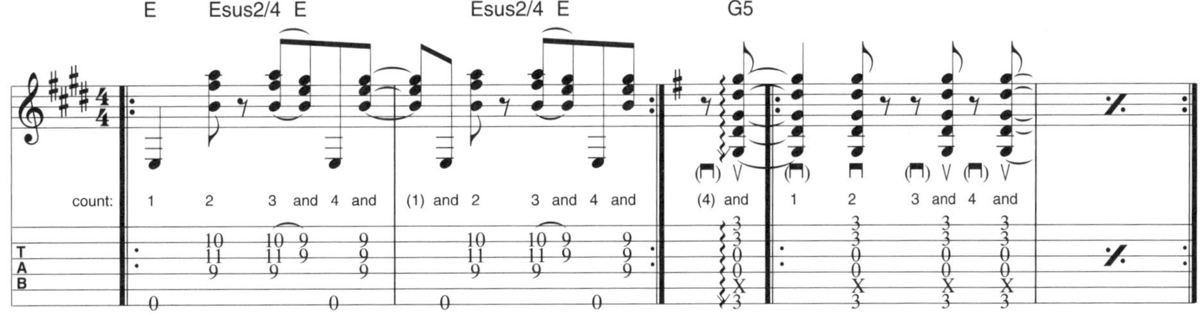

Keith Richards relied heavily on open-*G* tuning for his post-'60s rhythm guitar style. His trademark I–Vadd9 voicings in Ex. 14c—almost rhythmically identical to Ex. 14a—virtually define the Stones' sound from the '70s to the present. You can extend this rhythm figure by adding similar movements to *A♭* (barred at the 1st fret) and *B♭* (barred at the 3rd fret) as a means of reapproaching the tonic *C*. Richards emulates Chuck Berry in Ex. 14d, a pumping I–IV shuffle punctuated by jangly upper-register *A* and *Asus2* chord stabs.

Ex. 14c

Open G tuning (DGDGBD)

E♭ A♭add9/E♭ E♭ C Fadd9/C C A♭

count: (4) and (1) and 2 3 (and) (4) and etc.

Ex. 14d

Standard tuning

B5 B6 B5 A Asus2 E5 E6 E5 E7 E5 E6 E5

1 and 2 and 3 and (4) etc.

The Who were the power-pop antithesis of both the Beatles and the Stones. Supercharged bursts of rhythm similar to Ex. 15a took on a life of their own as signature intro and verse riffs. In turn, these had a profound effect on a generation of up-and-coming American counterparts, including a young Todd Rundgren. Example 15b, derived from a Nazz classic, cleverly restructures Ex. 15a's rhythm and embellishes its *D* and *A* chords, but there's little disguising its origin.

Ex. 15a **Ex. 15b**

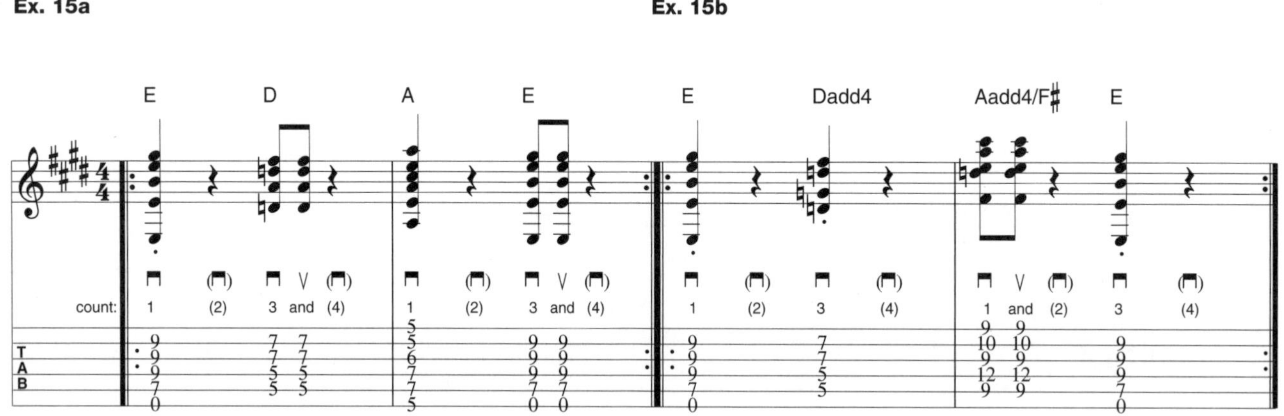

After the Who and Cream raised the bar with heavier rhythm guitar sounds, bands on both sides of the pond—from Led Zeppelin to the James Gang—picked up the ball and ran with it. Bombastic power-chord-based rhythm figures began appearing in many bands' repertoires. Examples 16a–16c provide a glimpse of three related sonic assaults. Try playing them in various fretboard positions using different chord voicings and transposing them to different keys.

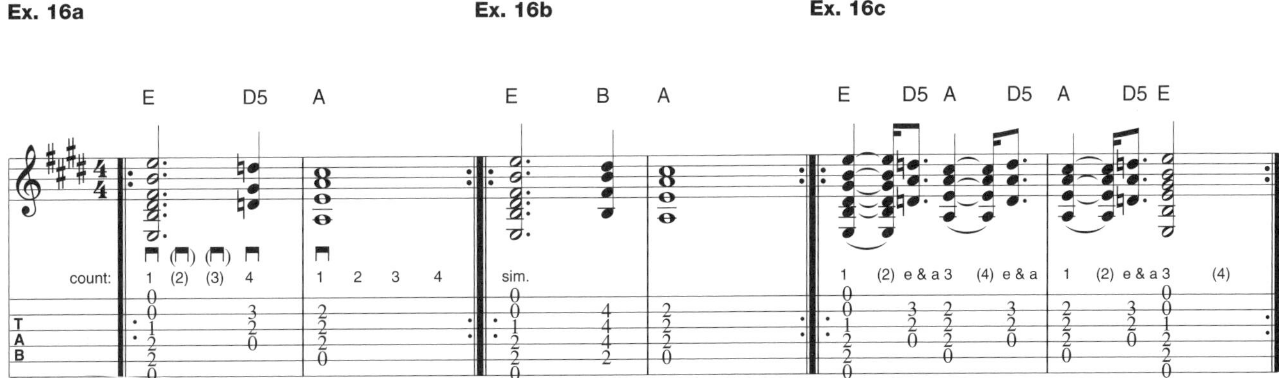

The arrival of Jimi Hendrix certainly shook things up for the Brits. From self-contained proto-metal riffs that sounded like an entire rhythm section to delicate R&B-influenced excursions of exquisite beauty (more on those in a minute), Hendrix displayed a magic touch that redefined rhythm guitar playing. His chords seemed to sound bigger and more powerful than everyone else's, probably due to the fact that he tuned his guitar one half-step below standard tuning and often fretted the low *E* string with his thumb. Hendrix's roots in the R&B chitlin' circuit and his penchant for the 7#9 chord—known to many as the "Hendrix chord"—led to dozens of signature rhythm guitar gems, such as the drumkit-meets-guitar riff in Ex. 17a and the bluesy call-and-response phrasing of Ex. 17b. Note the two different fingerings of the same *F#7#9* voicing, and be sure to quiver the one on beat *four* of Ex. 17b—it'll make your day.

*All notes and chords sound 1/2 step lower than written.

R&B, Soul & Funk

In the funky world of R&B and soul, rhythm guitar duties are often split into two or more parts. Example 18a plays fine as written, but if you assign the single notes to one guitar and the staccato backbeat chord "chiks" on beat *two* to a second instrument, you'll hear that magic Motown interaction come to life. Sliding 4th intervals like the ones in Ex. 18b played a big part in the rhythm guitar work of Curtis Mayfield, who, in turn, inspired Hendrix.

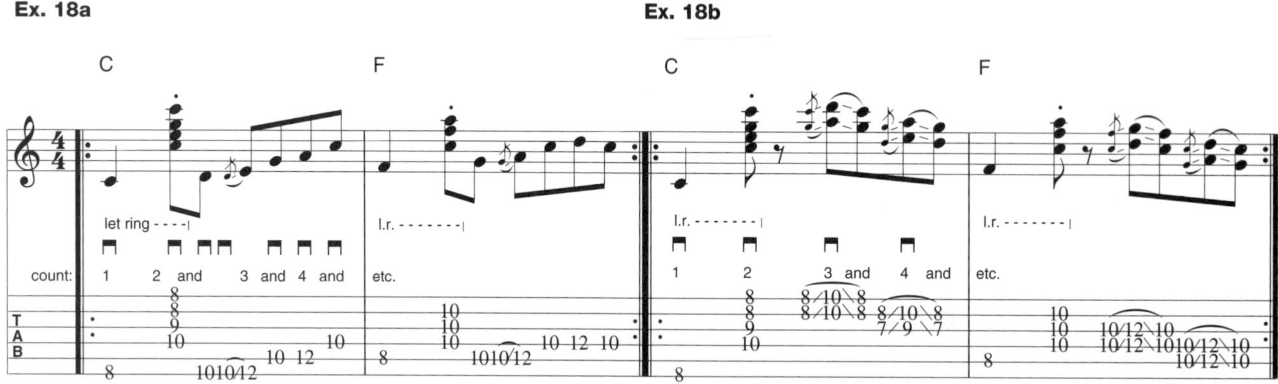

James Brown's funky soul always required a minimum of two guitars to overlap rhythm figures like the scratchy syncopated *E9* chords in Ex. 19a and the staccato single-note line in Ex. 19b.

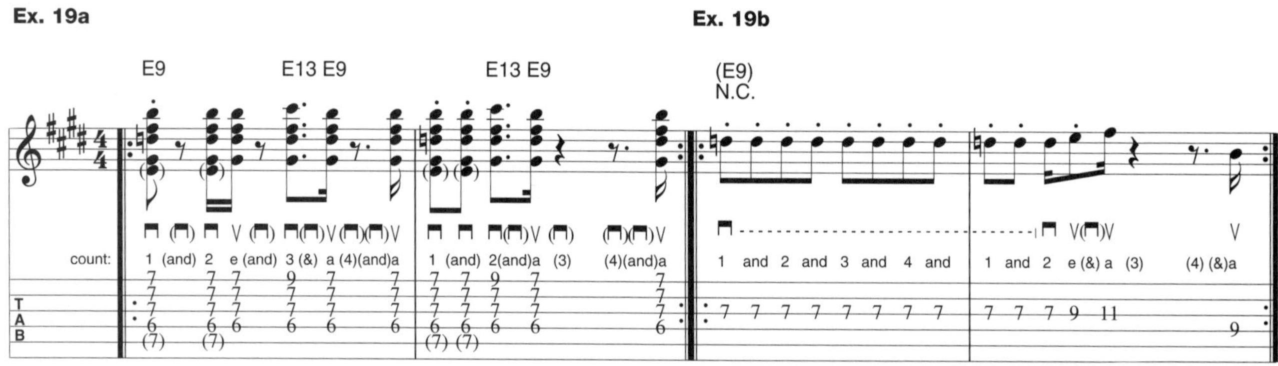

Hendrix's ballad style introduced a multitude of cool R&B moves built around a few standard barre-chord shapes. Example 20 crams thumb-fretted bass notes, sliding 4ths, hammer-ons and pull-offs, and jazzy chordal fragments into a two-bar *G–Am* progression.

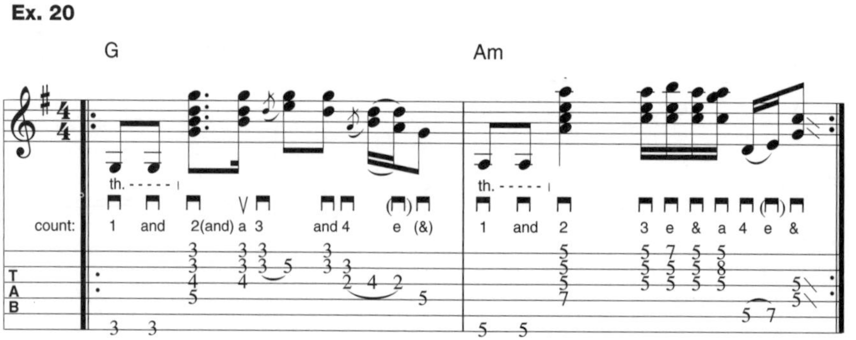

'80s Corporate Rock

Tragically, the guitar fell victim to the dreadful disco craze in the mid-'70s and was banished to a world of scratchy octaves, wah-inflected major-7th chords, and banal single-note "tick-tock" parts. Yeah, it was rhythmic, but let's forget it ever happened. By the late '70s, corporate rock had reared its ugly head in bands like Foreigner and Journey, and rhythm guitars were steered towards happier, shinier territory (Ex. 21a) or became overly sensitive and embarrassingly introspective (Ex. 21b).

'80s Hard Rock & Metal

All guitarists owe a debt of gratitude to Edward Van Halen—arguably the post-disco generation's closest heir to Hendrix—for bringing the public back to its senses. Credited as yet another reinvention of the instrument, Van Halen's lead playing has received the most acclaim, but he's also responsible for an armada of killer rhythm figures. Many of these—from "I'm the One" to "Jump"—are based on the type of pedal-tone and diad combinations found in Examples 22a and 22b (though Van Halen decorates his rhythm riffs much more extravagantly than your average headbanger).

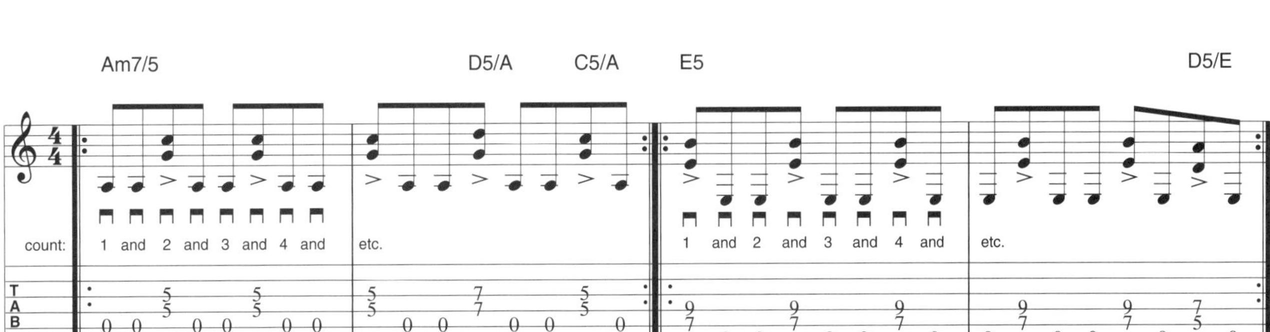

The heavy, galloping rhythms heard in most modern-day speed metal are apt to be some adaptation of the three rhythmic permutations shown in Examples 23a–23c. Though these rhythms are illustrated using octave *A* notes, you can adapt any chord or chordal fragment to each one. And once you get these three basic divisions of the beat down, it's easy to mix and match them, as in Examples 24a–24c.

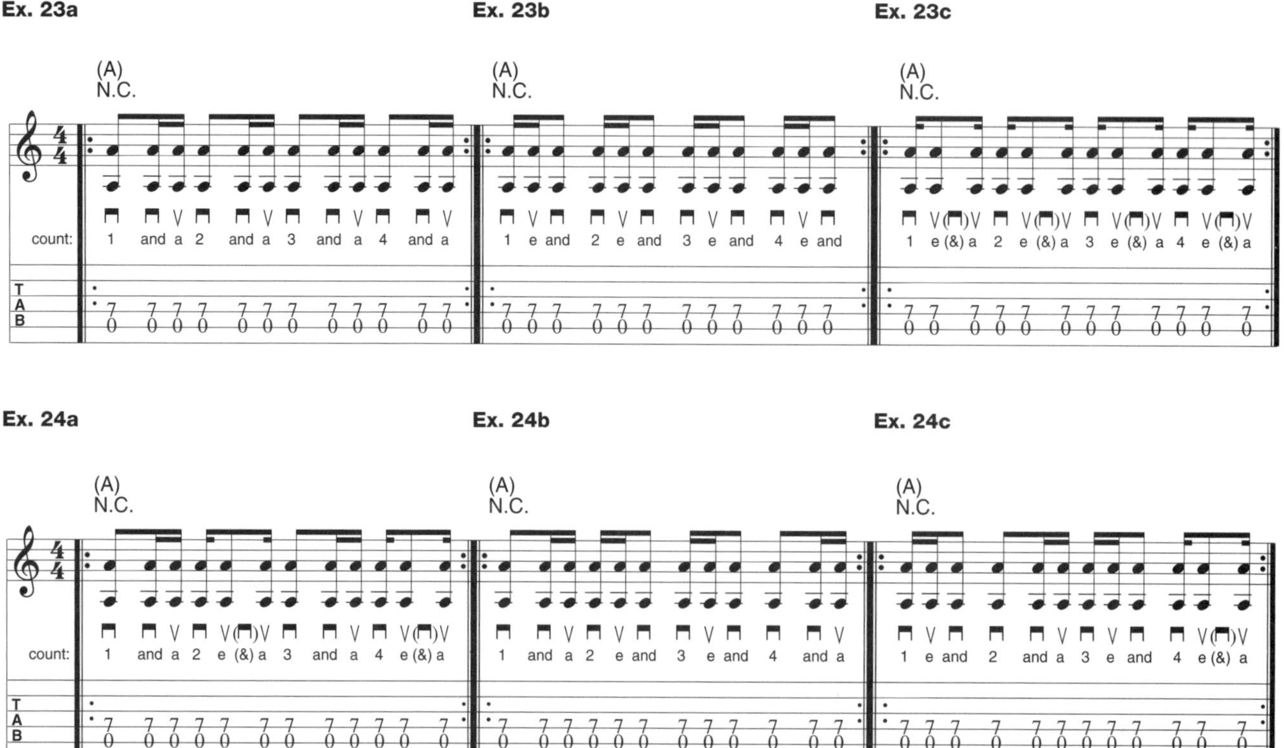

'90s Alternative/Corporate Rock

I'd love to end with a bang, but I'm still waiting for it. The '90s seemed to bring us full circle with a resurgence of mediocre, uninspired rhythm guitar, and it was hard for me to hang with what essentially amounted to a load of traditional folk rhythms on steroids, but it certainly resonated with the kids. Bands like Nirvana waved the flag for a new generation with the umpteenth version of "Louie Louie" (Ex. 25a) and influenced a sea of clones intent on delivering rhythms like the ones in Ex. 25b with as much ferocity as they could muster. Fill in your own chords—any will do.

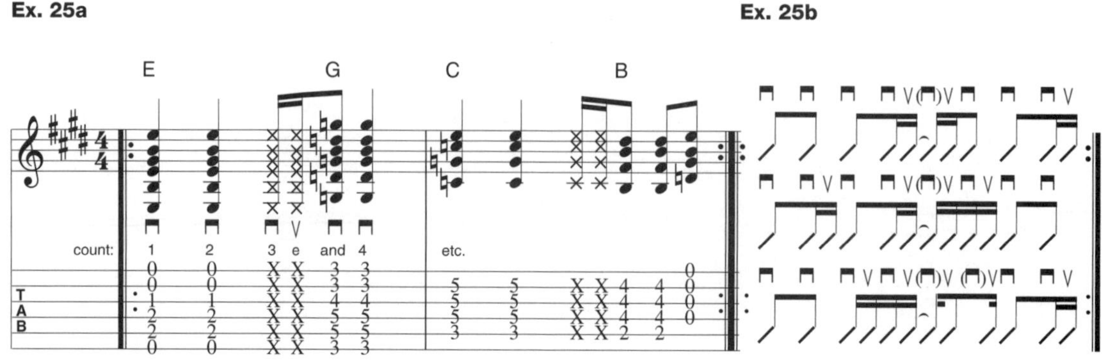

The turn of the century has brought a new hope to the instrument. The world is filled with more guitarists than ever before, and some damn fine ones at that. It's still too early to detect an all-encompassing new trendsetter or guitar savior, but who knows? Find the right combination of new sounds and it may well be you!

NOTES OF NOTE

Need to brush up on your rhythm basics? Now's the time. The following charts illustrate all basic note values and their rhythmic division into halves and thirds.

Note symbol	Note name	Note value	Rest symbol
	whole-note	4 beats	
	dotted half-note	3 beats	
	half-note	2 beats	
	dotted quarter-note	1 1/2 beats	
	quarter-note	1 beat	
	dotted eighth-note	3/4 beat	
	eighth-note	1/2 beat	
	dotted 16th-note	3/8 beat	
	16th-note	1/4 beat	
	32nd-note	1/8 beat	

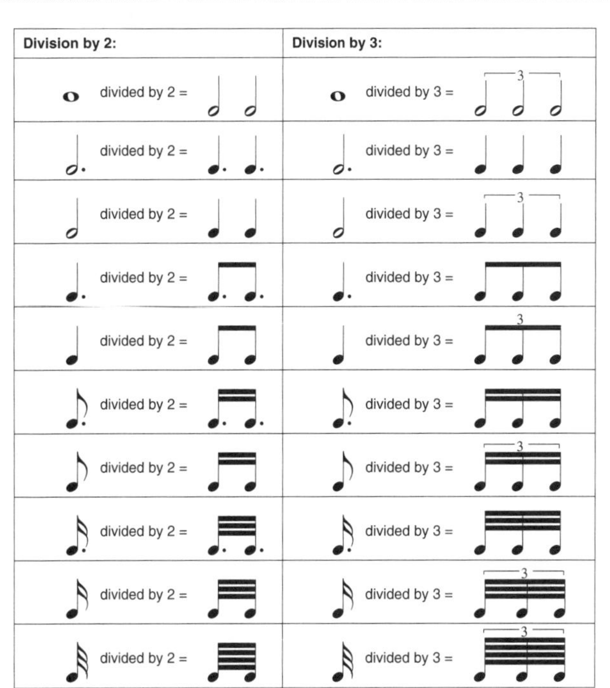

Division by 2:	Division by 3:
divided by 2 =	divided by 3 =
divided by 2 =	divided by 3 =
divided by 2 =	divided by 3 =
divided by 2 =	divided by 3 =
divided by 2 =	divided by 3 =
divided by 2 =	divided by 3 =
divided by 2 =	divided by 3 =
divided by 2 =	divided by 3 =
divided by 2 =	divided by 3 =
divided by 2 =	divided by 3 =

CHORDLESS COMPING

Play Kick-Ass Rhythm Using Intervals

BY ANDY ELLIS

When you hear the words "rhythm guitar," what leaps to mind? Crunchy power chords? Chimey open-string voicings? Perhaps you imagine jazz man Freddie Green's three-note swing grips, or Hendrix-inspired hammers and pulls that flow around partial-barre shapes like hot wax in a lava lamp. These sounds are all cool and essential, yet you can also play dynamite rhythm guitar without fretting a single chord. The secret lies in knowing how to use *intervals* to outline a progression.

In this lesson we'll explore ways to sketch rich harmony in a variety of styles—funk, blues, country, and jazz—using only intervals. Once you've investigated these examples, you'll have a new way to play *and* hear music.

First, we need to distinguish between a chord and an interval. A chord contains three or more notes, and an interval comprises two notes. An interval measures the distance—or air gap, as jazzer George Van Eps used to say—between two tones. You can play an interval harmonically (both tones at the same time) or melodically (one tone following the other). In these examples we're concerned with the *harmonic* interval—two notes sounded simultaneously.

An interval can't pack the same punch as a bigger voicing—it's a matter of physics. By sacrificing power, however, you gain mobility. Think about it: A five- or six-note chord is clunky—you can't dart around the fretboard with these huge blocks of sound. By contrast, an interval is nimble. Instead of strumming a fixed chunk of tones for one or more measures, you can use intervals to poke and jab at the harmony to create a more adventurous groove.

In practice, you'll find that integrating intervals *and* chords offers the best of both worlds. But for now, let's play a game—just how much music can we make using only two notes at a time?

Our interval palette consists of 12 half-step possibilities. We use two of these in Ex. 1, which alternates between tart major 2nds and sweet major 6ths, to create a funky groove. Played as written, the riff sounds angular and tight. If you want a grittier vibe, add 16th-note string scrapes during some of the rests.

This riff drapes nicely over a *D7*, *D9*, or *D13*, and because it doesn't use open strings, you can transpose it to any key. The secret to moving any riff lies in identifying its root (or, if the riff doesn't contain a root, visualizing its *assumed* root). In this case, the root (*D*) lies on the 3rd string—it's the top note in the insistent major 2nds.

As you shift positions, let your 3rd finger glide on the 4th string. *Feel* your way along the fretboard. To play great rhythm guitar, you need to take your eyes off the strings and watch your bandmates instead of your fingers. It's crucial to stay connected to the ebb and flow of the music around you, and you can't do that when you're absorbed with your own movements.

Ex. 1

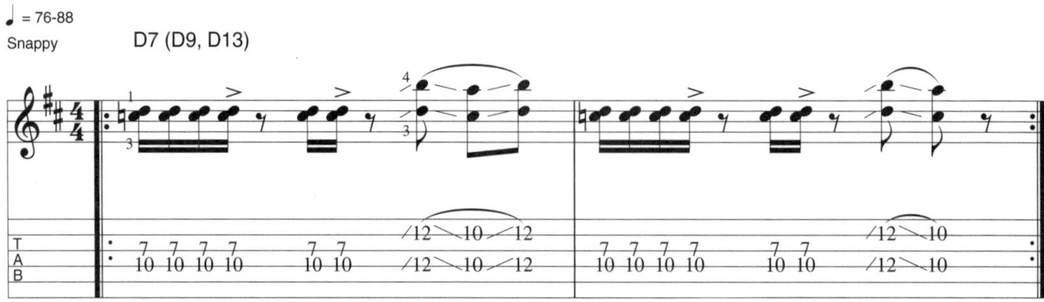

We stay in the same pocket for Ex. 2—a sassy call-and-response riff. It contains a major 3rd (*D–F#*), two different tritones (*C–F#*, *F#–C*), a minor 6th (*E–C*), and a 5th (*F–C*).

Those nagging tritones are at the heart of this one-bar groove. Beat *one* contains *C–F#*, our first tritone. The last interval in beat *three* is the second tritone, *F#–C*. Notice that it's simply an inversion of the first tritone. (To invert an interval, drop the top note an octave, or, conversely, raise the bottom note an octave.) A tritone is the only interval that remains the same when inverted. All other intervals morph into something else. For example, a 4th becomes a 5th, a 6th becomes a 3rd, a 2nd becomes a 7th, and an octave becomes a unison.

The next time you are jamming over a dominant-7th or dominant-9th chord, try our greasy Ex. 3. Here, it's notated as a *D7* move, but you'll have no trouble sliding this figure into other keys. It begins with Ex. 1's rhythm grafted to one of Ex. 2's tritones, and ends with a pair of major 3rds. The quarter bend in beat *four* adds a bluesy touch. That last *D* is optional.

Ex. 2

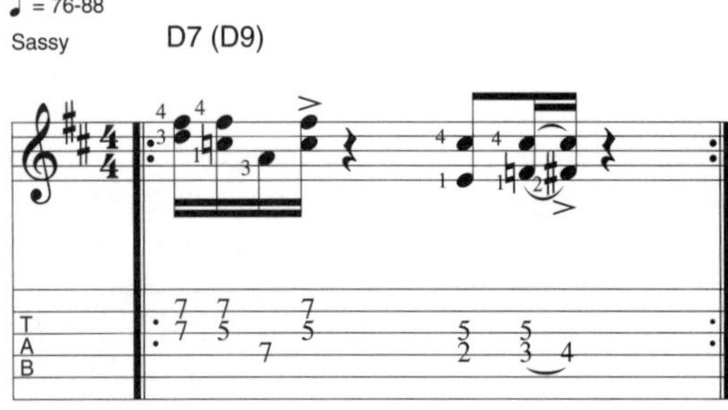

Ex. 3

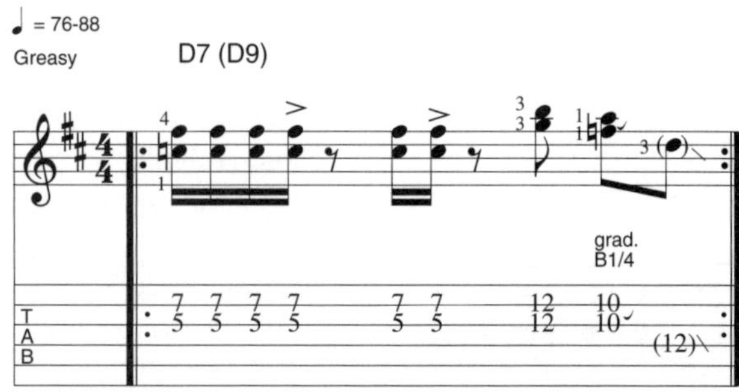

Ex. 4 mixes tritones and major 2nds into a sparse yet stinky groove. With its half-note rest, this lick illustrates the power of silence in rhythm work. It contains all the required tones to send the dominant-7th message—root (*A*), ♭7 (*G*), and 3 (*C#*)—yet you're fingering only two shapes. The sliding tritones in beat *three* imply a gospel-inspired IV7–I7 shift. These notes provide harmonic momentum, balancing the static major 2nds. This figure moves well along the fretboard, and, because it doesn't crowd the airwaves, it's handy for jams.

Ex. 4

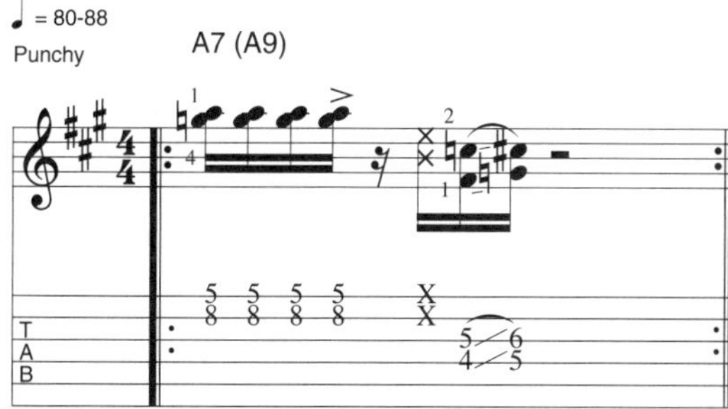

While we're on the subject of jamming, let's tackle the classic Don Rich comping pattern in Ex. 5. This is the single most important groove in honky-tonk. It's like a secret handshake—you need to know this twangy riff to step through the clubhouse door.

I've watched great hotrod Tele pickers—such as Albert Lee, Ray Flacke, and Johnny Hiland—play this lick, and they all barely move their fretting-hand fingers. The key is to roll back and forth between the partial barres played by your 3rd and 1st digits. For authentic snap, you *must* use a hybrid pick-and-fingers grip as notated. Pull the 2nd and 3rd strings up as you pluck them. You'll know you're doing it right when the 3rds start to pop. (See Notational Symbols, page 5, for an explanation of picking-hand notation.)

As shown here, it's a *C7* lick. By all means, identify the 3rd-string root and then start roaming the fretboard. Honky-tonk pickers typically use this pattern to comp a I–IV–V progression. Shift positions during the rest (bar 2, beat *four*).

Ex. 5

♩ = 152-176
Twangy C (C7)

The next two patterns come from the soul-blues family. As in the previous riff, Ex. 6a uses 3rds, but this time we're fretting a mix of minor and major shapes. See how the *D–F#* interval is first notated with the 3rd finger (beat *two*), and then with the 1st finger (beat *four*)? While you can play both intervals with either finger, this shared arrangement facilitates the position shifts—the 3rd finger ascends, the 1st descends.

In Ex. 6b, we keep the same four notes on the 2nd string (*E*, *F#*, *G*, *F#*) and harmonize it with a new line on the 4th string. Though it has the identical melodic contour as Ex. 6a, this new figure "weighs" more because it uses wider intervals—6ths. Use Ex. 6b when you need to fill harmonic space. In a large ensemble, the compact Ex. 6a would be more appropriate.

Both patterns are completely mobile. Try using a full dominant-7th barre (root on the 6th string) as a visual anchor. Once you can see these moves in relation to a barre *A7*, try moving up the neck to *D7* and *E7*. Congrats! You now have two flavors of a I7–IV7–V7 blues comping pattern that will work in any key.

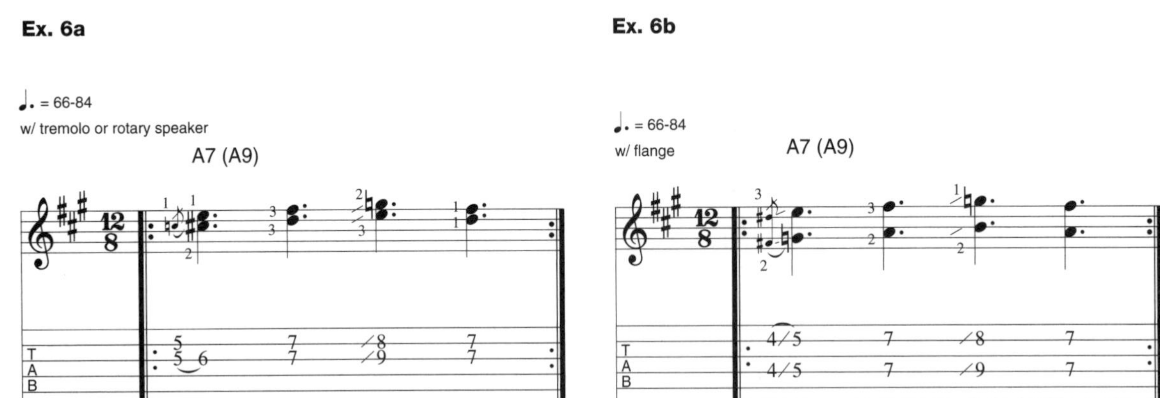

Master the art of inverting intervals, and you'll have twice as many accompaniment patterns at your disposal. For instance, take Ex. 7a—a festive line composed of major and minor 3rds. These intervals let you outline a progression—in this case, a I–V–IV–I in the key of *G*—while staying very melodic. As you move through the four chords, listen to the lower voice (it's on the 2nd string).

Now, try Ex. 7b. Here, we've dropped what was the higher voice down an octave so the 2nd-string line is the top voice. As mentioned earlier, when you invert 3rds, they become 6ths.

Thirds evoke a mariachi band, and 6ths emit a country or Memphis R&B vibe. Thirds are compact, 6ths are wide, and both sounds are essential to chordless comping.

In each phrase, the intervals on beats *one* and *three* contain the root and 3rd from the chord of the moment. On the other beats, the intervals shift between chord tones and non-chord tones. The latter are piquant passing tones that beg for resolution, while the former reinforce the harmony.

Ex. 7a

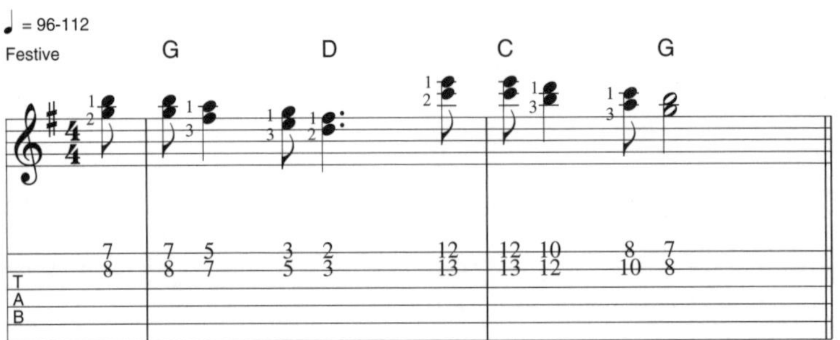

Pay attention to the fretting-hand fingering and notice how one digit stays in contact with the string for the entire passage. In Ex. 7a, it's the 1st finger that functions as a guide, while the 2nd finger assumes this role in Ex. 7b.

Ex. 7b

Jazz's mainstay progression is the venerable IIm7–V7–Imaj7. It's easy to sketch this cadence using intervals, as you'll see in Ex. 8. Here, we're playing a lively two-bar samba rhythm during the IIm7–V7 change, but you can mate these intervals with virtually any beat and tempo.

Ex. 8

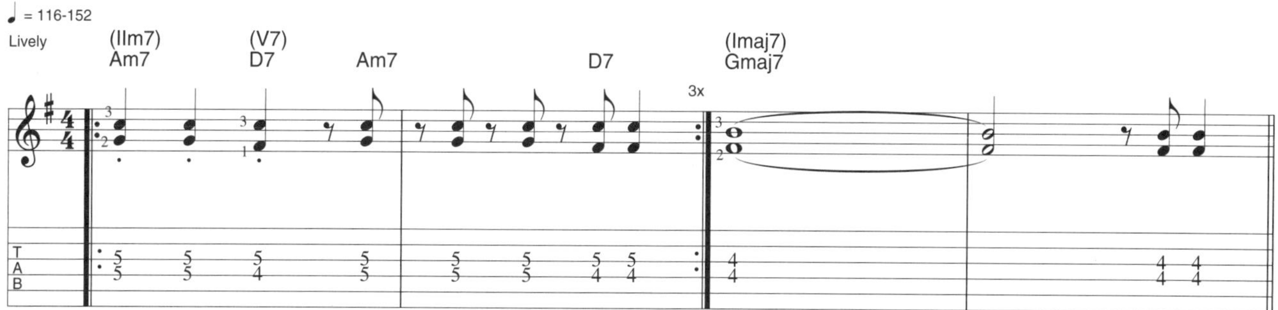

Here's an idea: Move the IIm7–V7 portion through different keys before you finally hit the Imaj7. For example, try back-cycling in 4ths through the keys of *A*, *D*, and *G*, using the syncopated samba rhythm and interval shapes shown in Ex. 8.

- First, play *Bm7* and *E7* (IIm7 and V7 in the key of *A*) in the 7th and 6th positions.
- Next, move to the 12th and 11th positions to play *Em7* and *A7* (IIm7 and V7 in the key of *D*).
- Finally, drop down to the 5th and 4th positions to play Ex. 8's *Am7*, *D7*, and *Gmaj7* figures.

Repeat each IIm7–V7 segment (for a total of four bars) before switching to the next key. If you record these changes, you'll have a snappy and challenging accompaniment for practicing melodic improvisation. To give yourself ample time to explore these three keys, try tracking the entire back-cycling extravaganza three or four times in a row.

The groove in Ex. 9a works equally well for big-band R&B, raunchy Chicago blues, or funky, organ-driven soul-jazz. Give each interval its full value—you want a sustained, legato sound—and let your 2nd finger glide along the 4th string as you shift positions.

Here, we've notated the groove as a compact V7–IV7–I7 change in the key of *A*, corresponding to bars 9, 10, and 11 of a 12-bar blues. It's up to you to unsnap each bar, reconfigure the moves into a full 12-bar progression, and add a turnaround of your choice in bar 12. (Need some turnaround ideas? See Blues Boomerangs: 12 Essential Turnarounds in Backbeat's *How to Play Blues Guitar*.) Once you've done this, be sure to drag these moves into several other keys.

Ex. 9a

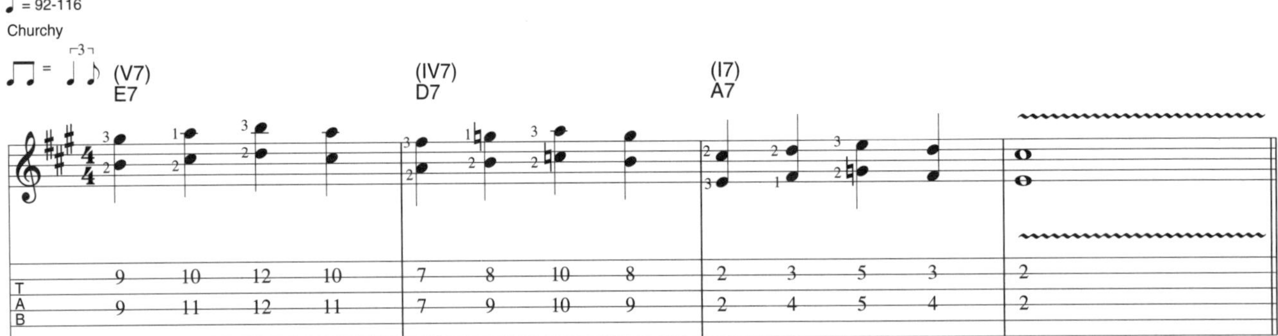

Ex. 9b shows how to finger the same soulful 6ths on strings 3 and 5, instead of strings 2 and 4. If you memorize both sets of shapes, you'll have two locations to play this groove in any key. The trick is to visualize the starting chord's assumed root.

- When you're cruising on the 2nd and 4th strings (as in Ex. 9a), the unplayed root lurks on the 3rd string. It's located on the same fret as beat one's two fingered tones.
- When you're squeezing the 3rd and 5th strings on beat one (Ex. 9b), the silent root lies on the 4th string, sharing the same fret as the lower voice.

Ex. 9b

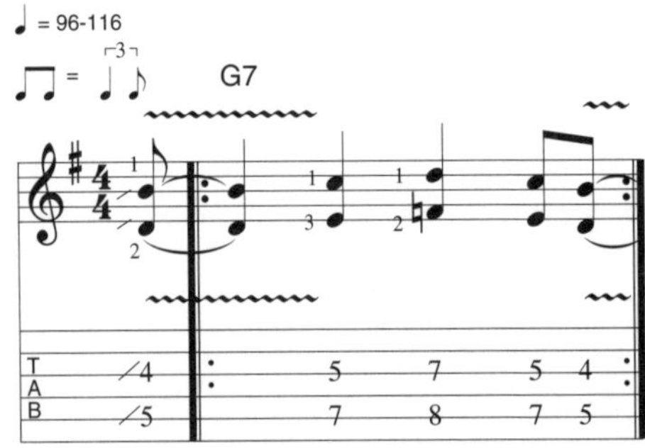

How would we cope without power chords? The classic power chord is, of course, composed of the root and 5 played on wound strings. But there are other options besides the resulting 5th, as evidenced by Ex. 10, which includes 4ths and a 6th. The interval changes are subtle, but they add momentum and drama to what would otherwise be a static part. Add some crunchy distortion, palm-mute the bass strings, and gradually bring the riff to a boil.

Ex. 10

Now let's honor Bo Diddley with—*whoa*—power 7th chords. Example 11a shows his namesake beat, the classic "shave 'n' haircut, two bits" rhythm. Typically, you'd pound this out using open-position chords—*A* and *D* or *E* and *A*. Those I–IV changes sound super with the Bo Diddley beat, but as a scratchy alternative, try Ex. 11b. With some subtle palm muting, you can choke the strings and turn your guitar into a wiry percussion instrument. Add some fast tremolo and you'll have a swampy groove that suggests a dominant-7th chord, yet leaves plenty of room in the higher registers for other instruments or vocals. We're fretting the root and ♭7 of *A7* (*A* and *G*) and *G♯7* (*G♯* and *F♯*).

Ex. 11a

Ex. 11b

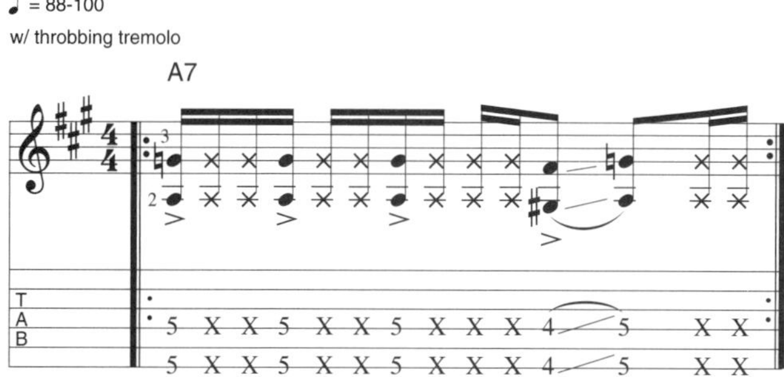

In Ex. 12a we juggle two lines. Composed of eighth- and 16th-notes, the top line is melodic, while the bottom line plays a supporting role and sticks to quarter- and half-notes. Heard together, these lines create a complex series of intervals that range from a major 2nd (*A–B*) to a minor 7th (*F♯–E*). Pop and country ballads often feature this type of ornate melodic accompaniment over a strummed acoustic background. Try this with a smidge of reverb and some slow, subtle tremolo. Make sure you sustain the low notes for their full value.

Ex. 12a

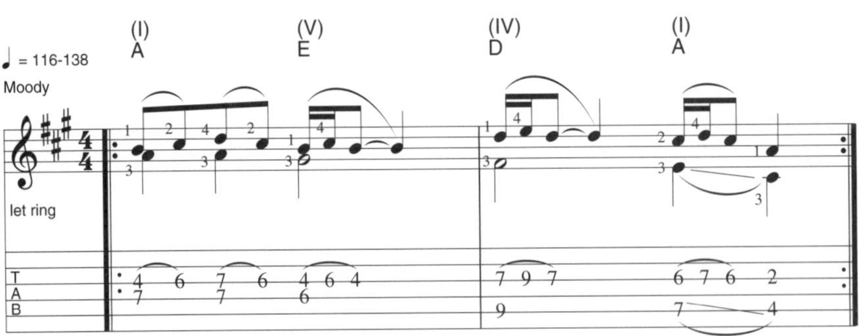

Example 12b features the stirring sound of sliding 4ths and the lonesome twang of 4ths hammered into 3rds. The surprise comes in bar 3, where you ascend using a mix of intervals: perfect 4ths, major 6ths, a major 3rd, and a minor 6th.

Bar 4 features a bona fide pedal steel lick. To nail the first half, you need to set up a perfect-5th prebend and then relax back to a minor-6th shape. A steeler would use a pedal to change the minor 7th (*E–D*) in beat *three* to a minor 6th (*F♯–D*), but on the 6-string a gentle hammer-on does the trick.

Ex. 12b

As we've seen in these examples, rhythm parts composed of intervals can be graceful or gnarly, tangy or sweet. Ironically, the more you learn about constructing chords, the easier it is to comp without them. Once you adopt a "no chord" mindset, you'll start hearing harmony in a new way. Small horn sections are a good source of inspiration, as are vocal duets. Perhaps the most compelling feature of the guitar is its ability to express both singing melodies and big, chiming harmony (pianos don't sing, and saxes can't comp). Chordless comping splits the difference between these two musical extremes and puts a third option at your fingertips.

TRACKING THE AIR GAP

An interval is the distance in pitch between two notes. We measure this distance in half-steps, as shown in the Common Intervals chart. You'll notice that some intervals have more than one name. Called enharmonic intervals, these sound the same but are named differently according to the musical context. For instance, you may hear the space of six half-steps as a perfect 5th that has been made smaller (diminished), or as a perfect 4th that has been expanded (augmented).

To streamline the list, we've chosen not to show less common enharmonic intervals (such as the diminished 3rd, which is equivalent to a major 2nd, or the diminished octave, which equals a major 7th). Instead, we've stuck to the interval types you'll encounter on a daily basis.

Compound intervals are larger than one octave. To determine the essence of a compound interval, simply subtract seven. A major 9th, for example, is a major 2nd plus an octave (9 – 7 = 2). A minor 10th is a minor 3rd plus an octave (10 – 7 = 3). Compound or not, an interval's quality (major, minor, augmented, or diminished) stays the same.

Common Intervals

interval name	half-steps
unison	0
minor 2nd	1
major 2nd	2
minor 3rd	3
major 3rd	4
perfect 4th	5
augmented 4th	6
tritone	6
diminished 5th	6
perfect 5th	7
augmented 5th	8
minor 6th	8
major 6th	9
minor 7th	10
major 7th	11
octave	12

BUSTIN' LOOSE

13 Pathways to Cliché-Free Rhythm

BY ANDY ELLIS

It's harder to be a great rhythm player than a hotshot lead guitarist. In a solo, you can dance across the band. Playing rhythm, you churn its bones. While you can pause to get your bearings during a lead break, you'd better not drop the ball on a groove. Rhythm guitar kicks your musical ass every step of the way.

Some songs demand a steady barrage of big chords, but often the opposite is true: When you break free of clunky five- and six-note forms, the music breathes. The trick is to maintain momentum—arguably the single most important ingredient in any rhythm part—while juggling smaller harmonic elements in ear-tweaking ways.

For instance, take a two-bar *E7–A7* progression (Ex. 1). It doesn't get simpler, right? With a little imagination, you can turn an otherwise boring set of changes into a rocking riff. The tritone—an interval of three whole-steps—forms the heart of a dominant-7th chord. Notice how in bar 1 the tritones for *E7* (beat *two*) and *A7* (beat *three*) lie a half-step apart. We can take advantage of this phenomenon to create some greasy one-fret chord changes. (Funk and R&B horn players routinely work this I–IV tritone axis.) Alternating fretted tritones with a palm-muted open 6th string lets you ride two registers and play off contrasting timbres. Watch the vibrato markings: In bar 1, wiggle *A7*'s tritone with your fingers. If you've got a trem bar, use it on the next bar's *A7*. Such subtleties spell the difference between ho-hum and hot damn. Try a bright, slightly gritty single-coil tone.

Example 2, another two-chord pattern, illustrates how you can combine simple triads and space to create a compelling rhythm part. Rather than repeat the same *Em* and *Am* forms every two bars, here we use inversions to create a four-bar phrase and thus increase harmonic interest.

Ex. 1

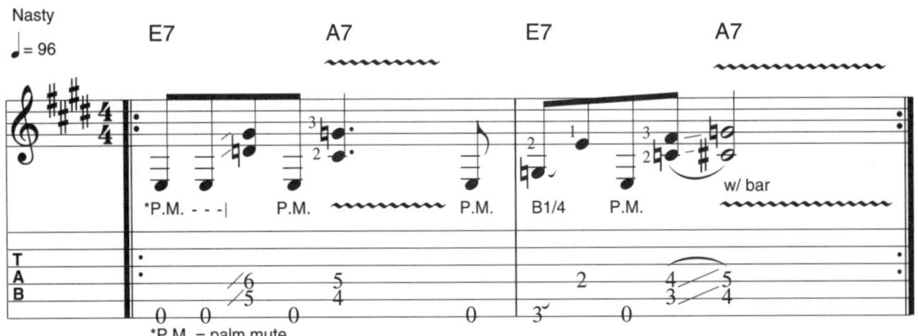

It's also slick to create wheels within wheels. Check out how the open-string figures set up a two-bar call-and-response against the four-bar chord pattern. Those recurring rests produce rhythmic tension by offsetting moments of sound with a 16th-plus-a-beat's worth of silence. Accents on the second chord and last note of each bar highlight the syncopation. It's all in the details.

Ex. 2

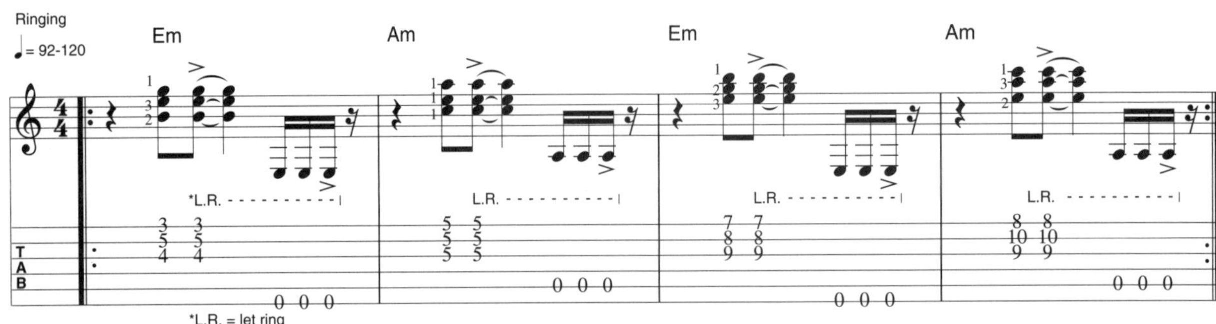

Imposing a given rhythm across a series of chords, as in Ex. 3, is an excellent way to develop a hooky part. In each arpeggio, two beats of pluck precede two beats of ring. Such yin/yang construction keeps the ear engaged. Because a rhythm part demands forward motion, however, we can't just nod off during the last half of every measure. Use a twang bar (or gently manipulate your guitar's neck) to keep each sustaining chord pulsing, however subtly. The contrasting open-string and fretted timbres keep each voicing fresh. This part sounds nice played clean with a dab of reverb.

Ex. 3

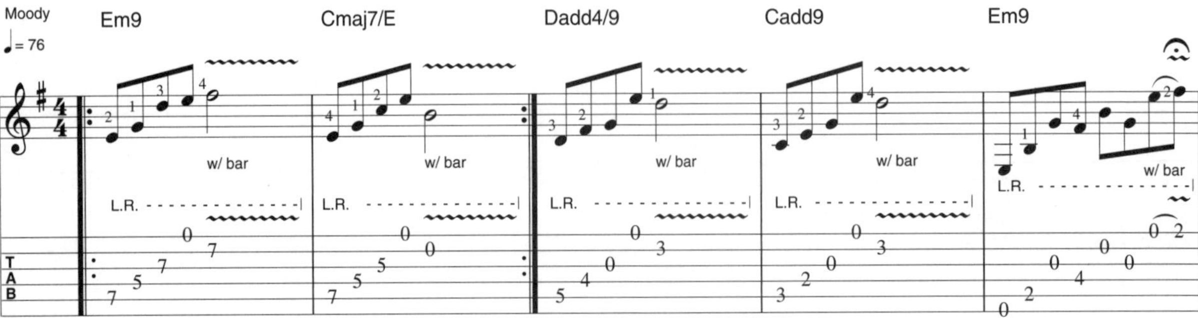

It's fun to riff with harmonically ambiguous 4ths and 5ths. Is it major? Is it minor? Example 4 explores this territory in the context of dropped-*D* tuning. Bar 1 contains the kind of Austin-inspired *D–G* power-chord interplay that rocks a country tune so well (think David Grissom). Containing both a 5th and a 4th, the one-finger power chords in bar 2 make a meal in themselves. You could write a dozen kicking riffs from this one simple voicing. For starters, play bar 2's power chords backward. Then turn the line inside out and add some new fret positions. Use a wah to emphasize those muted chords: *dadah–wacka–dadah.*

Try a hybrid pick-and-fingers approach: Snap bar 1's 4ths and 5ths with your middle and ring fingers and flatpick the single-note riff and bar 2's barre chords. Tonally, aim for a Tele crunched to the edge of chaos.

Ex. 4

Speaking of Teles, Ex. 5 is the sweetest R&B riff this side of Memphis. It offers the 5th, 6th, and ♭7th found in Chuck Berry's bass-string rhythm patterns, but in descending order. Lean on the muted scratch at the downbeat of each bar. Emphasize the slides and carefully articulate those quick hammers. This riff should roll with a continuous eighth-note pulse. Don't interrupt its steady flow when you change chords—the muted scratch lets you keep the train a-rollin' while your fingers find their frets.

Ex. 5

Funk folks typically feature dominant 9th and dominant 7♯9th chords. But next time you're jamming, stir it up with a dominant 13♯9. Example 6a shows two voicings for the secret funk weapon. (Memorize each form in relation to its assumed root, shown as a hollow circle a whole-step up from the chord's lowest tone.) Example 6b puts that sucker in context. Each bar starts by sliding into an *E7* tritone from a half-step below. The snappy *E13#9* to *E9* change (bar 1, beat *three*) is classic James Brown. Bar 2 introduces another chord on beat *three*. Comprising stacked 4ths, it functions here as an *E7sus4*. Use it as a sub for *E7* whenever you seek harmonic ambiguity or an edgy, restless feel.

Ex. 6a

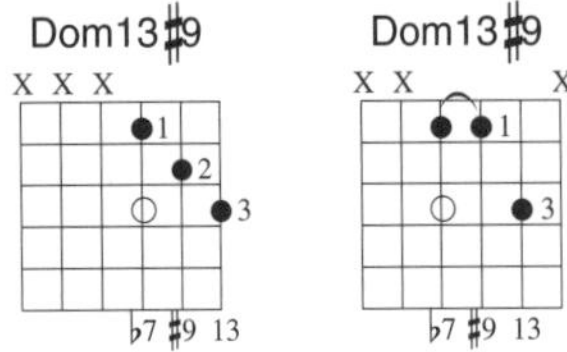

○ = assumed root

Ex. 6b

Greasy

♩= 92-112

The dominant-13th voicing in Ex. 7a is guaranteed to stamp an uptown vibe on your blues and R&B. Shown here as an *A13*, this four-note form has a ♭7 in the lowest voice. Notice how this chord is conveniently sandwiched between *D9* and *E9*, its IV7 and V7 companions. The voice-leading possibilities become mind-bending when you approach any or all of these chords from a half-step above or below. With a major nod to T-Bone Walker, Ex. 7b offers a

Ex. 7a

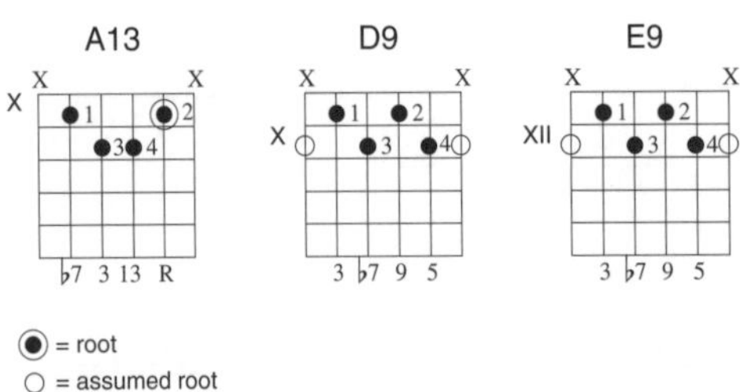

● = root

○ = assumed root

taste of the chromatic delicacies you can cook up with just these three forms. Here, we've dropped into the final bars of a 12/8 blues. Experiment with other keys and watch the assumed roots.

Ex. 7b

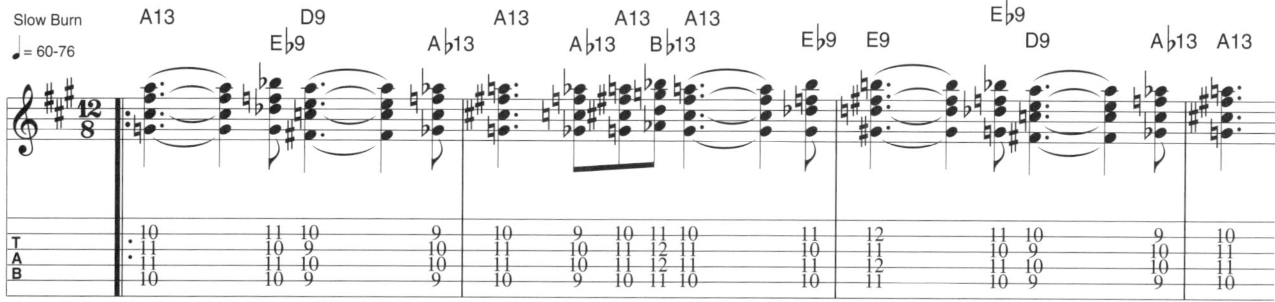

Example 8 shows how useful triads can be in a funky rock groove. They're small enough to be mobile—and thus let you stage melodic moves—yet fat enough to strum. In bar 1, notice the subtle difference between sliding into an *A7* tritone from below (beat *one*) and hammering from an *Am7* to *A7* ("and" of beat *two*). Learn both approaches—they're indispensable. The muted skritches are as important as any notes in this part. It's about drive: In a rocking riff, don't let the pulse flag while you shift fretting fingers from one grip to the next.

Here's a fingering tip: Sometimes you'll want to barre the *D* triad with your 3rd finger (beat *two*, bars 1 and 2), sometimes with your 1st (bar 1, beat *four* and bar 2, beat *one*). It comes down to positioning yourself for any upcoming action. Always experiment when developing a part, since the right fingering can make the difference between stumbling or sailing through a set of changes.

Ex. 8

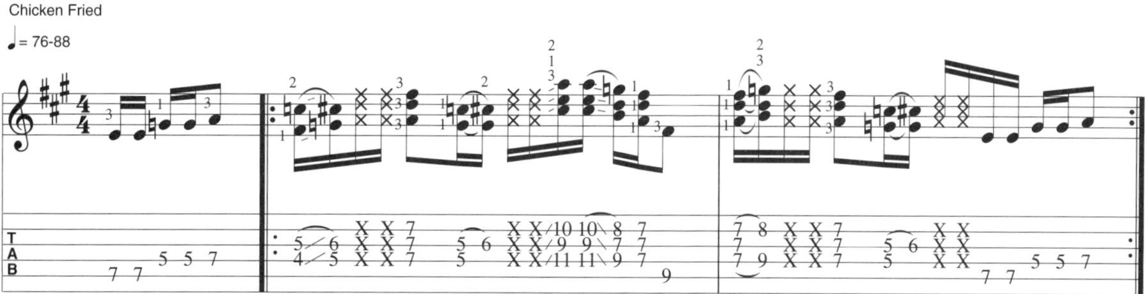

Fingering is crucial in Ex. 9—another funky, beer-drenched R&B riff. In bar 1, we play the identical notes back to back (beats *two* and *three*), but finger them differently—first with the 1st finger, and with the 3rd. This fingering unlocks the riff like a skeleton key. Dig the major 2nds in bar 2. Playing the ♭7 and root together creates a delightful rub. It even stands alone as a funky, stabbing rhythm part. Add the ♭7–6 resolution ("and" of beat *four*, bar 2) for yet another cool R&B module.

Ex. 9

Ex. 10a shows three dominant-7th voicings that exploit major-2nd dissonance. You won't find these in garden-variety chord dictionaries, but rest assured they are to swampy rock and R&B as salsa is to a burrito.

To get rolling with these forms, try Ex. 10b. In bar 1, let those *F*'s and *G*'s ring together à la Billy Gibbons. Put some grind in your tone. The trick is to dial in enough gain to make the major 2nds sound tough, but not so much that they disappear in the murk. (By the way, when amp shopping, use these voicings to test a model before buying. Some amps make distorted dissonance sound groovy. Others just crap out on major or minor 2nds and 7ths. Tritones are also excellent for testing amps. Teeth-on-a-sidewalk ugly? Dirty sweet? When you have the opportunity, check out a blackface Fender Deluxe and an original Vox AC30 to calibrate your ears to two types of distorted dissonance.)

Cop the turnaround in the last two bars and try it in other bluesy contexts. Dig the stepwise voice-leading (strings 3 and 4) beneath the *G* common tone.

Ex. 10a

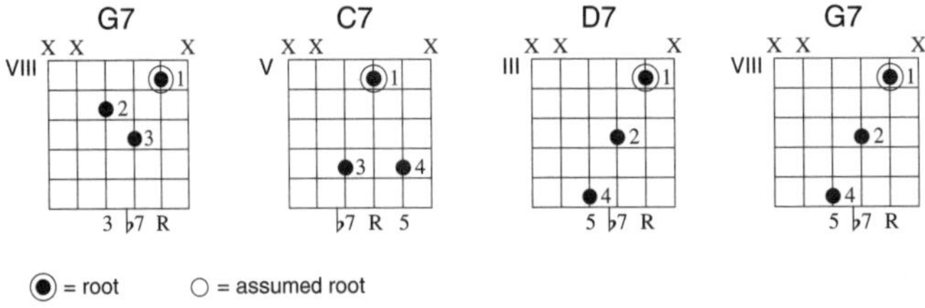

Ex. 10b

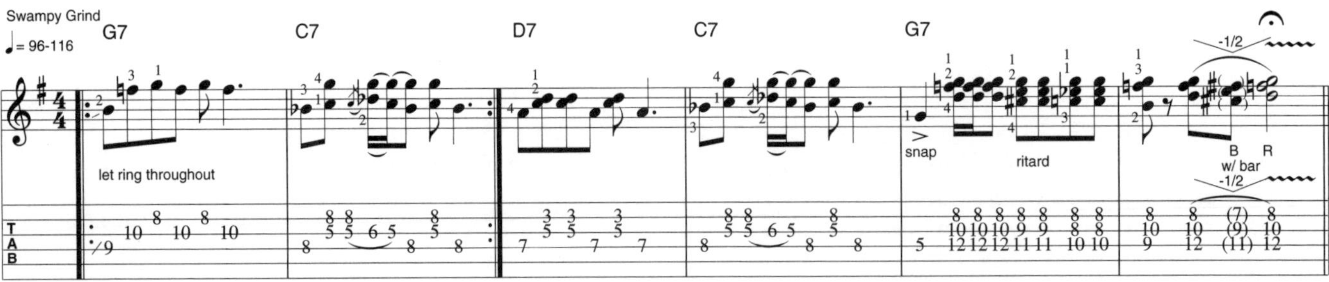

The high-*A* common tone that runs through Ex. 11 binds the chord sequence together and sets up a call-and-response pattern with the repeating low-string riff. As the inside harmony moves against the backdrop of these recycling motifs, we sense the connection between one chord and the next. Note the voice-leading—it's stepwise until the final chord.

Beat *two*'s accents impart a reggae flavor to the groove. To create the muted skanks, release—but don't remove—your fretting fingers from all notes except the top *A*. Let the string tension bounce you up and off the frets.

Ex. 11

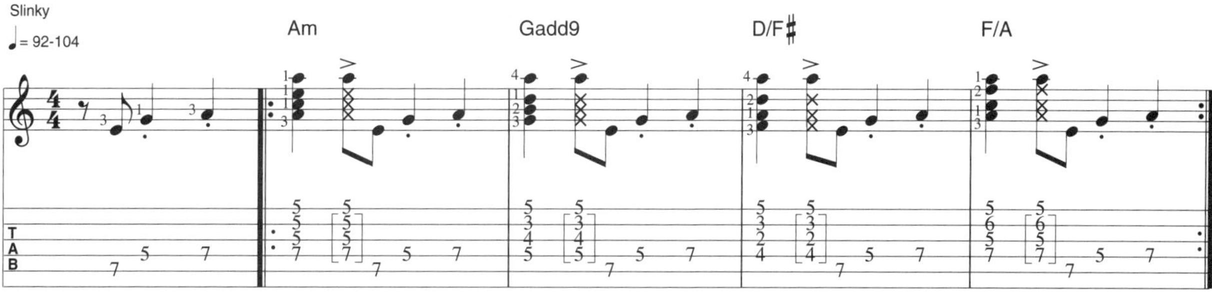

As we've discovered, a rhythm part usually benefits when you contrast repetition with change. Example 12 features two themes that repeat in each measure of this four-chord progression. The first is a rhythmic scheme that anticipates each upcoming chord by an eighth-note, yanking us across the barline into every new change. The second is the five-note melodic motif that occurs on beats *two* and *three*, and the downbeat of *four*. The harmony evolves against this fixed structure. Open chords provide many opportunities for such internal themes. When writing an open-chord rhythm part like this, look for physical moves you can repeat within each grip.

Ex. 12

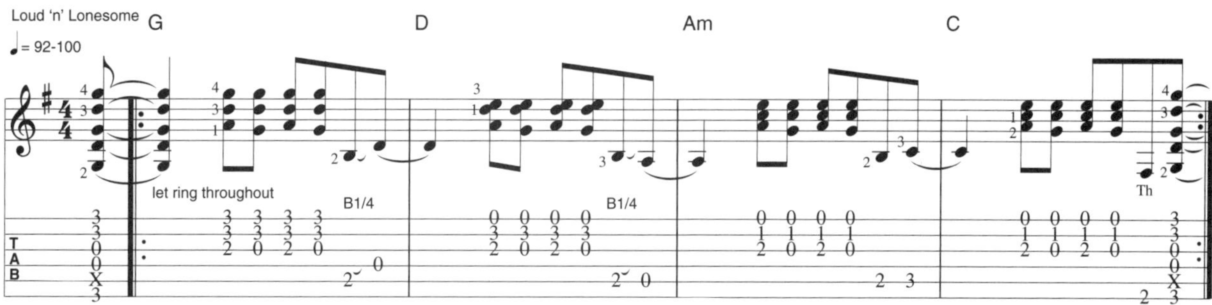

No rhythm lesson would be complete without celebrating the melodic approach pioneered by Curtis Mayfield and perfected by Jimi Hendrix. When working out Ex. 13, listen for:

- Suspended-4th to major-3rd resolutions
- Hammers and pulls between a major chord and its relative minor
- Major chords with their 3rd in the bass
- Slides into these low 3rds
- Hammers and pulls to and from the 2nd and 3rd chord tones.

Strive for a fluid, ringing sound—a Strat's neck pickup does the trick—with a touch of reverb or modulated delay. Isolate the moves in this example and apply them to other chords and keys. It takes time but yields magic.

Ex. 13

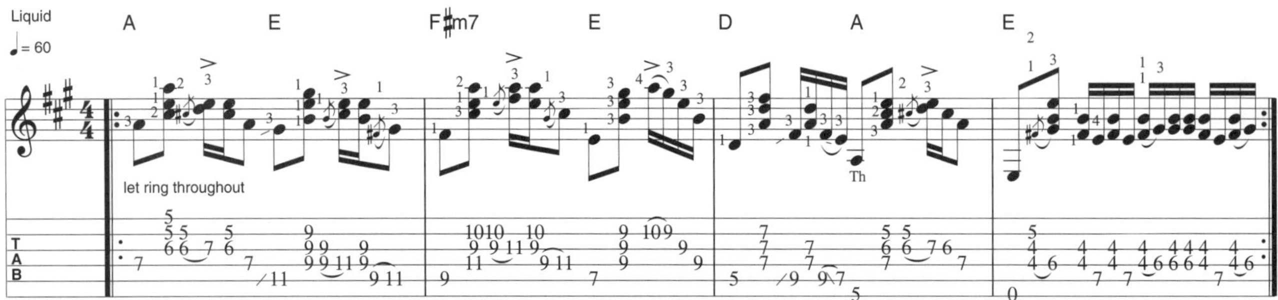

As you play these examples, hunt for the techniques they embody. Work these ideas—syncopation, anticipation, call-and-response, tension and release, tritones, drones, and voice-leading—into your own grooves. Balance dissonance with consonance, silence with sound, and repetition with change. Internalize these concepts and your rhythm chops will never be the same. Nor will your lead playing: Nailing rhythm guitar will raise your soloing to a new level—guaranteed.

BLUES: SHUFFLE POWER

Hip Rhythms & Smoky Substitutions

T-Bone Walker

BY DAVE RUBIN

The shuffle is like a human heartbeat. Whether played on drum or string, those two swinging eighth-notes duplicate the timekeeper of life. A great shuffle is so fundamentally stimulating that foot-tapping becomes an unconscious response. Listeners who wouldn't know a blue note from a blue heron will still groove to shuffle-based tunes like "Kansas City" and "Everyday I Have the Blues."

Shuffle rhythms go back at least as far as the music of early 20th-century Delta blues pioneer Charley Patton. In the '30s Robert Johnson mesmerized juke-joint crowds with shuffles such as "Sweet Home Chicago" and "Dust My Broom," in the process drafting the rhythmic blueprint for postwar Chicago blues. Swinging Kansas City bands such as Count Basie's added jazz improvisation to their sophisticated 12-bar arrangements during the big-band heyday of the '30s and early '40s. And '50s R&B singer Big Joe Turner hit the pop charts with songs like "Shake Rattle and Roll," thinly disguised shuffles masquerading as rock 'n' roll.

But for most blues guitarists, the shuffle age begins around 1940 with the mighty T-Bone Walker. The first in a long line of swinging Texas electric guitarists, T-Bone passed the torch to such Lone Star legends as Gatemouth Brown, Freddie King, Albert Collins, and Stevie Ray Vaughan. Meanwhile, Chicago and New Orleans players developed their own idiosyncratic shuffle styles.

In this lesson we'll look at six examples of shuffle rhythms that can help you authenticate your blues comping credentials. Some are notated in 4/4 with directions to play the eighth-notes in swing rhythm; others are notated in 12/8 with three eighth-notes per beat. In either case, you should feel the examples as having four beats per measure and play them at a comfortable medium tempo.

Example 1, "Texas Shuffle," is your basic garden-variety 12-bar pattern. Notice, however, that the chord forms add distinction with their bright, brassy voicings. The *D9* with *C* in the lowest voice, in particular, bleats like an R&B horn section. The transition to the *G9* in bar 5 is smoothed by the common *D* note, and bars 9 and 10 cop a jazz guitar trick: As the *A9* moves to *G7,* the common *G* and *B* notes are retained, but the 4th-string *C#* moves up to *D,* the 1st-string *E* to *F.* The voicing ascends, even though you'd tend to think of the V chord as moving *down* to IV.

Ex. 1

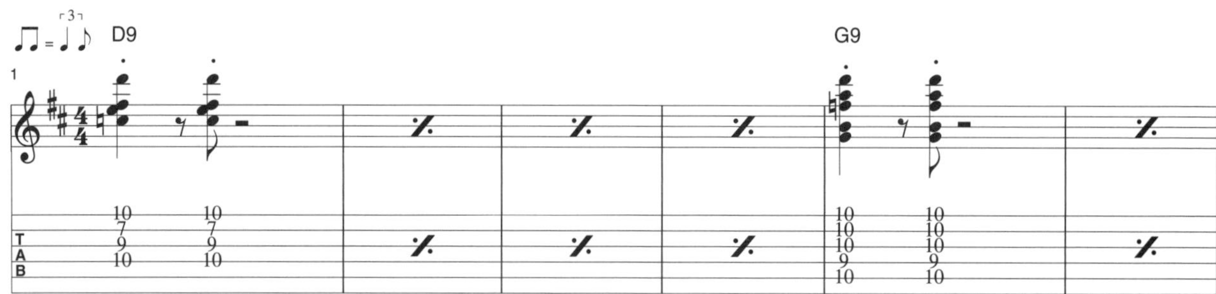

Many shuffle voicings are derived from horn parts. Example 2, "Billy Butler Blues," is based on the sort of horn charts that T-Bone, Gatemouth, and B.B. King liked to blow over. (Billy Butler is the great blues/jazz guitarist who contributed those three perfect choruses to organist Bill Doggett's "Honky Tonk" in 1956; I once heard him use these types of added 6th and 9th voicings to comp behind Big Joe Turner.) In a hornless rhythm section, this type of progression provides a smooth pad for singers or soloists. Think of horns gliding effortlessly between chords as you gliss into each change, applying steady left-hand pressure to achieve

Ex. 2

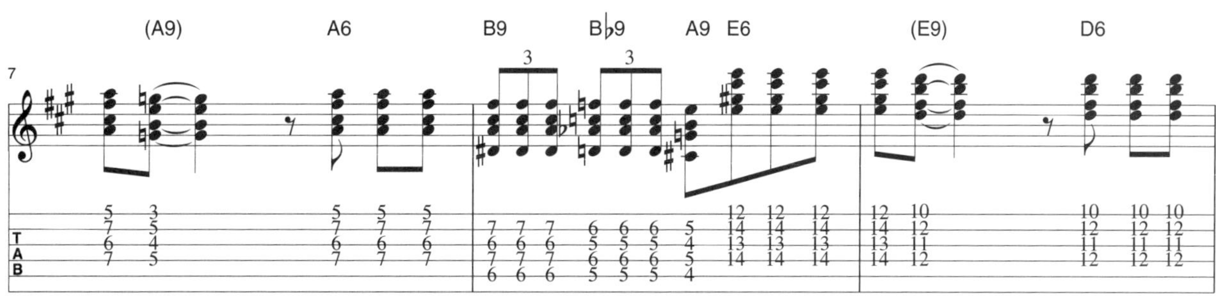

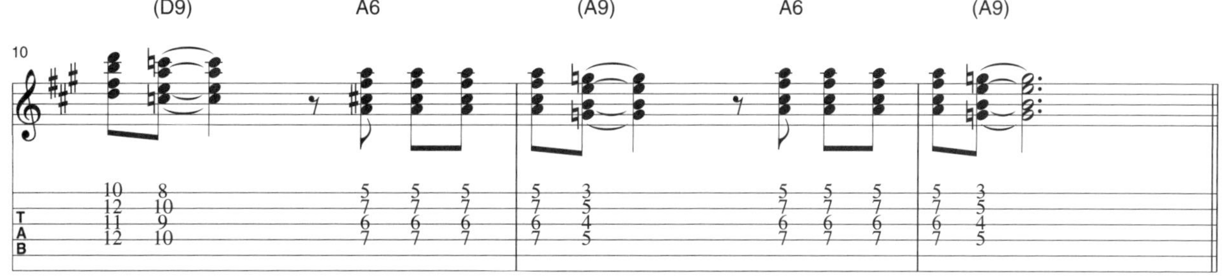

(D9) A6 (A9) A6 (A9)

the desired legato effect. The 6th chord leading to an inverted 9th (bars 1, 2, 3, 7, 9, 10, 11, and 12) are a blues-hip and cool addition to your chord arsenal. You can also omit the 1st-string root, especially if the root is supplied by a bass player. And dig the slick trick at the end of bar 3, where *A6* becomes *B9* in bar 4 by simply moving your 1st finger from the 1st-string *A* to 5th-string *D#*. The *B9* resolves through *B♭9* to *A9*.

Ex. 3

The unique syncopations in New Orleans blues come from the city's Caribbean and Latin influences. Example 3, "The 14-Bar Crescent City Blues," pairs a rumba-type rhythm with a swinging shuffle beat; similar patterns occur in the piano playing of Professor Longhair, Dr. John, James Booker, and Allen Toussaint. The example gains its extra two bars by extending the V and IV chords in bars 9 and 10 of a normal 12-bar blues. The Mixolydian double-stops are a bitch to play at anything above a relaxed medium tempo. I suggest using all down-strokes with strong staccato accents (and a bowl of gumbo for the right attitude). And if that 1–3–5 lick in the last two bars sounds familiar, you've probably heard it in the New Orleans rock 'n' roll of Fats Domino, Lloyd Price, and Huey "Piano" Smith.

The next two examples are based on the most popular shuffle rhythm pattern—"four on the floor," or four quarter-notes per bar. Example 4, "Jimmy Rogers Shuffle," is based on the kind of rhythm guitar accompaniment Rogers contributed to many classic Chess recordings of Muddy Waters and Little Walter.

Play the "dead string" *F7, F13,* and *B♭7* chords (bars 1, 3, 5, 7, and 11) with the left-hand thumb holding down the 6th-string bass note. This places your fretting hand in an excellent position to embellish the chord forms. It also leaves your 2nd finger free to hammer the ♮3 on the *G* string and your 3rd finger free to play grace-notes and double-stops. The technique is blues-approved and looks cool as hell.

Bars 7 and 8 feature a slick substitution copped from jazz. Instead of a straight I chord *(F)*, bar 8 uses the IIIm7 chord and then slides through ♭IIIm7, which leads nicely to the V chord in bar 9. T-Bone's "Stormy Monday" employs a similar substitution, as do some of the blues numbers on Robert Jr. Lockwood's *Steady Rollin' Man*. Also note the moody *B♭m6* subbing for the *B♭7* in bar 6 and the extremely gnarly chromatically sliding dominant-9th chords in bars 9 and 10.

Ex. 4

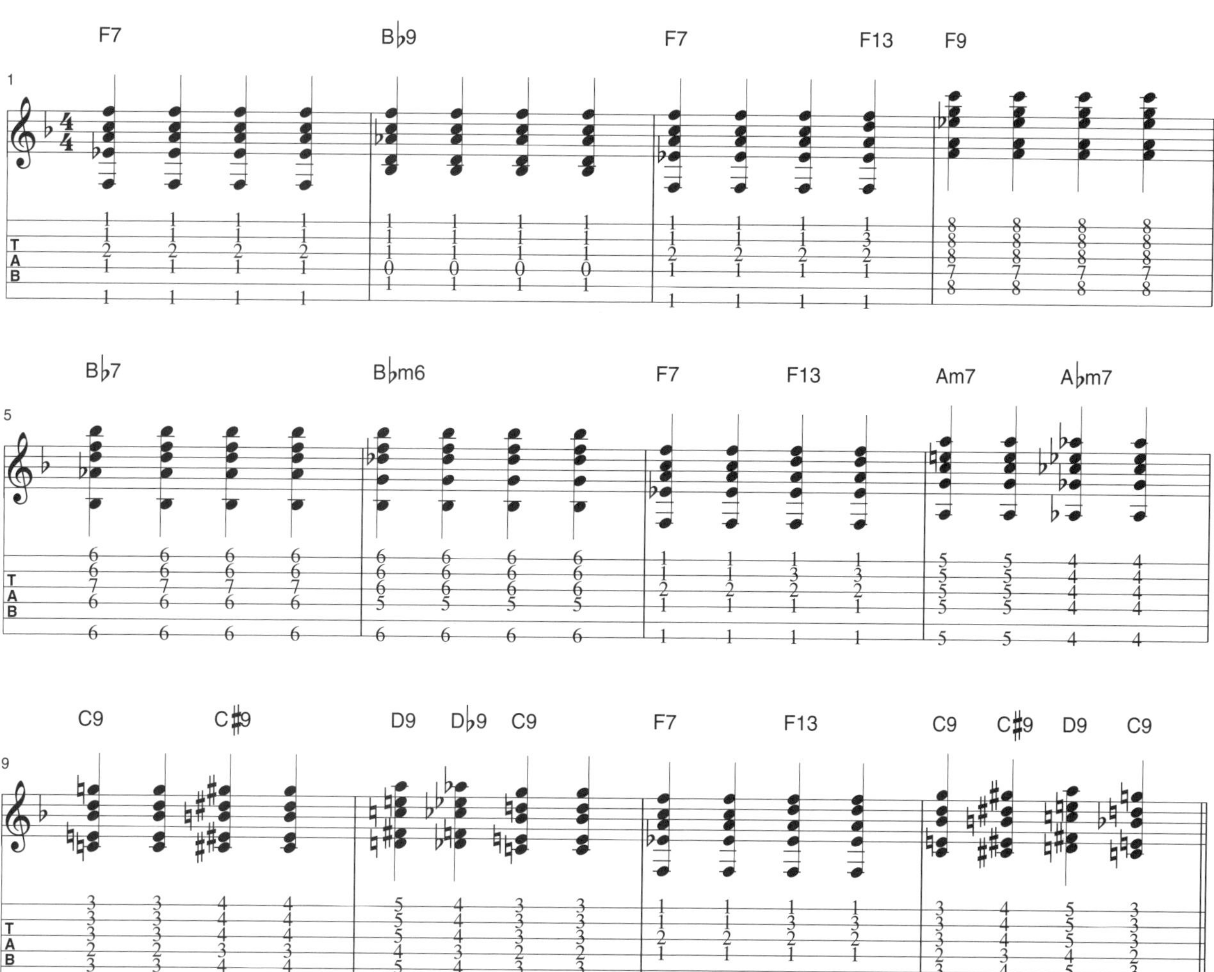

Example 5, "Roy Gaines Blues," is a jazzier version of Ex. 4. Gaines is an underrated Texas guitarist whose playing reveals the influence of T-Bone plus Johnny and Oscar Moore of Charles Brown's and Nat King Cole's bands. Robben Ford, Duke Robillard, and Larry Carlton sometimes swing in a similar way.

Ex. 5

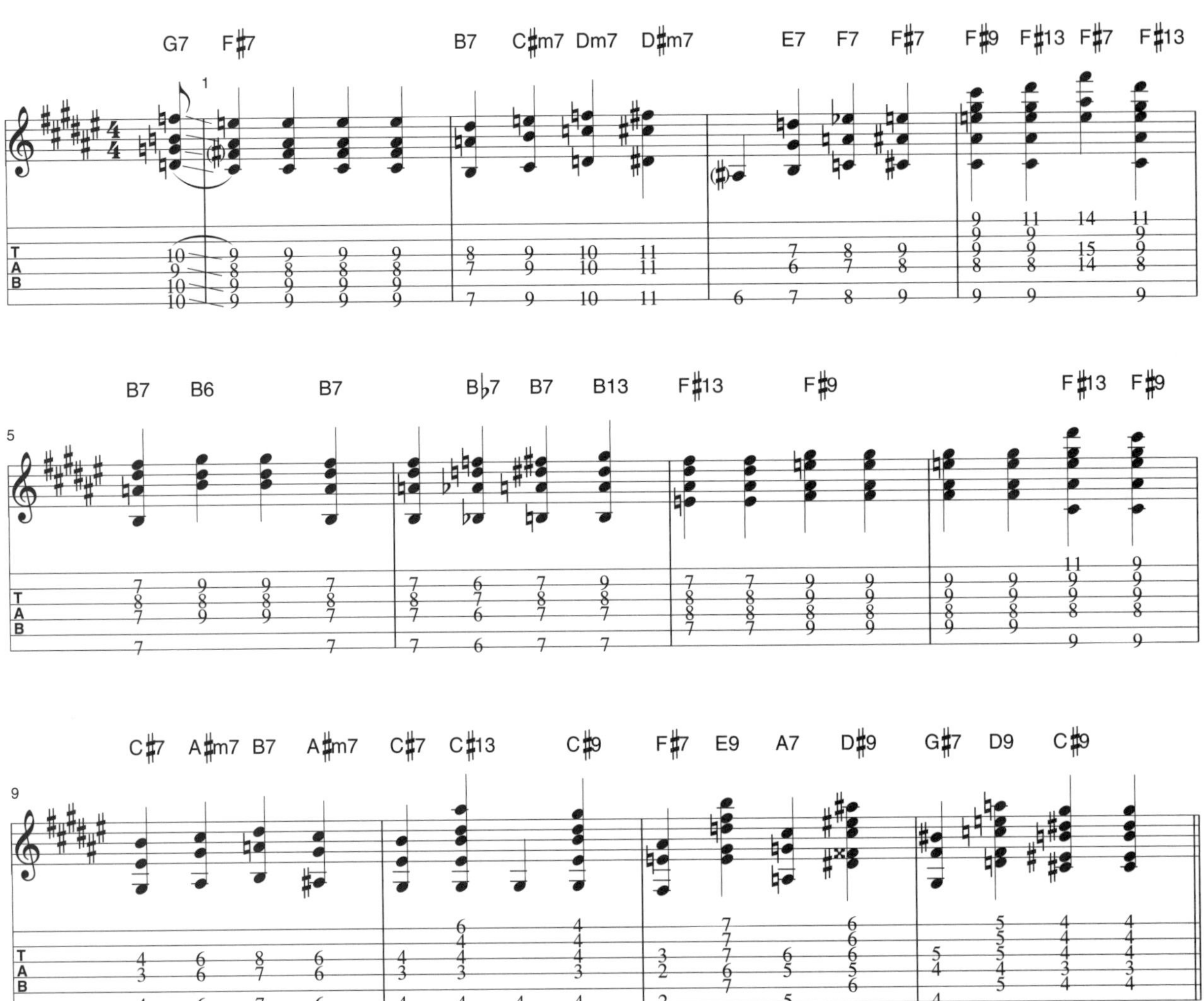

Bar 1 is the only straight measure in the progression. Bar 2 features a chromatically ascending series of minor-7th substitutions. The three-note dead-string voicings used throughout this progression are common to blues and jazz. Bar 3 really starts to motor as a walking bass line is harmonized with dominant-7th chords. Bar 4 layers on some melody with different *F#* dominant chords. The IV change in bars 5 and 6 is standard fare, save for the blurring of the bar line as the *B7* is held over from the beat *four* of bar 5 to the beat *one* of bar 6.

Four dominant voicings hold down bars 7 and 8, the bar line again blurred by the retained *F#9* chord. Check out that dandy *F#13* inversion with *E* in the bass; in another situation it could be combined with the *B9* voicing in bar 8 of Ex. 2 for a lush I–IV change. Bar 9 has some wild substitutions for the V chord (*C#*), anchored in turn by the steady *C#* dominant of bar 10. The turnaround in bars 11 and 12 combines walking bass with circle-of-4ths and tritone substitutions. The I *(F♯)* moves down to ♭VII *(E)*, but then shifts a 4th to *A*. Next, a cycle of dominant chords leads us down to *C♯*. The traditional blues practice of applying dominant chords to any and all scale degrees helps highlight the bite of the blue notes (♭3, ♭5, and ♭7) when improvising.

Ex. 6

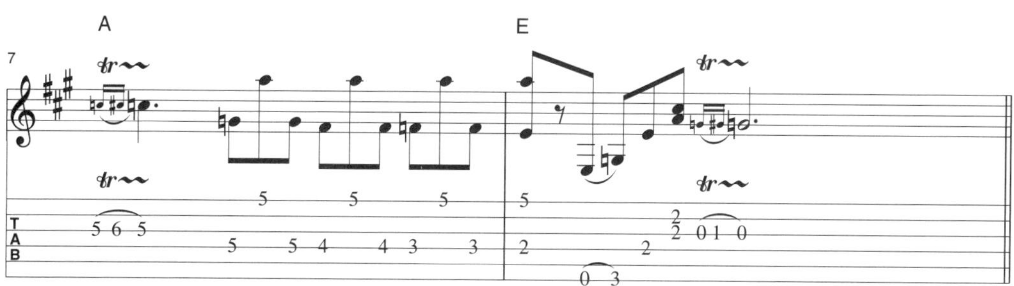

Example 6, "Highway Blues," is an eight-bar progression. The last and most rhythmically complex of our six shuffles looks back to the earliest-known forms of Delta blues guitar accompaniment. Its basic chord pattern can be found in many classic blues tunes, including "Key to the Highway." Here you'll find double-stops, walking bass, full and partial chord voicings, and lead fills—all the raw materials for the self-accompanied guitar improviser.

Bar 1 begins with an open 5th double-stop followed by a "hammered 3rd" (♭3–♮3) fill and an *A* arpeggio. This sort of bass line/chordal accompaniment occurs everywhere from Robert Johnson to Jimi Hendrix. Bar 2 more or less repeats bar 1 over the V chord, the second hammered-3rd lick played between the 5th and 6th frets to facilitate the move to 5th-fret *D9* in bar 3, which is followed by a walking chromatic bass line in bar 4.

Bar 5 chugs along in the solo blues bag, the open *A* droning beneath the following arpeggio lick with its harmonized 6ths. The Chicago-style shifting 9th-chord fragments in bar 6 fill out the harmony over the sustaining *E* bass string. The turnaround in bars 7 and 8 begins with a trilled 3rd (*C–C#*) followed by a standard Robert Johnson turnaround lick. The final riff emphasizes the blues' major/minor ambiguity. Freddie King uses similar figures on the heads of killin' instrumentals like "Wash Out" and "Heads Up." Check out the blues stylings of jazz greats Kenny Burrell, Pat Martino, George Benson, and Cal Collins for more ideas.

FUNK: RHYTHM METHOD

A Top-Down Funk Tutorial

BY ADAM LEVY

Prince

Funk is not an easily defined commodity. Sure, your handy-dandy dictionary may offer a few explanations for funk or funky: "having a musty smell"; "earthy and uncomplicated"; or "relating to music that has an earthy quality reminiscent of the blues." But do these phrases get anywhere near the crux of the biscuit? The two latter definitions certainly aren't wrong, but that "earthy" quality needs to be coupled with a danceable beat to qualify as "funk." Add "sensual" and "syncopated" to our definition, and we're starting to get a little warmer—though maybe the dictionary would best serve its readers by just reproducing a photo of Nile Rodgers next to the F-word.

When it comes to defining funk rhythms for the guitar, there are several schools of thought: Rodgers' slick chord moves, the salty grooves laid down by Funkadelic's many guitarists (including Tawl Ross and Phelps "Catfish" Collins), the skin-tight chanks of James Brown vet Jimmy Nolen, and Prince's downright nasty strumming. And these days, funk is almost inescapable—it permeates rock (Red Hot Chili Peppers), folk (Ani DiFranco), jazz (John Scofield), and jam bands (Galactic), and it has launched all sorts of hyphenated, hybrid musical strains.

So if you're looking to put a little funk in whatever style of music you play, we're here to throw down a few essential tips on funkification with a little help from Avi Bortnick, who has been working in San Francisco funk bands since the genre's late-'70s heyday. Recently his profile was raised considerably when he began touring with John Scofield's band in support of the leader's groovacious *Bump*.

"Initially I hired Avi to cover the rhythm parts I overdubbed on *Bump*," says Scofield, who has never before toured with a rhythm guitarist. "I wasn't looking for another soloist, but someone who lives in the rhythm guitar world. Avi does—he has that perfect, snapping groove with a relentless pulse, and he's funky. He also understands how all of the parts of a band work together—that's how he's able to do his thing so right."

Before digging into the nuts and bolts of funk guitar, let's take a minute to look at picking-hand technique—specifically the way you hold the pick. Not that there's any one "right" grip, but since playing funk rhythm is very different from playing lead, a different technique might be appropriate.

"For any funky sort of rhythm playing," says Bortnick, "I hold the pick between my thumb and my index and middle fingers, and my wrist is a little closer to the floor than usual. This grip lets your wrist move more freely and with a wider range of motion than the common down/up picking position. You get a little more power and snap. Also, gripping the pick with two fingers helps me hold onto it while I'm playing rhythm—I strum pretty hard."

So hard, in fact, that Bortnick installed Graph Tech String Saver saddles on his Strat to reduce the inevitable string breakage. "I still break some strings," he says, "but that comes with the territory. There's a sound you get from hitting the strings that hard—the whole guitar pops, and that's what you want. Also, when the strings are being struck that hard, you really feel it in your fretting hand, and one big thing about rhythm playing that most people don't get is that half of it comes from your fretting hand. That hand is not just forming the chords, it's doing a lot of muting. Without muting, funk guitar just wouldn't happen."

Fretting-hand muting is an essential skill for funksters at any level. We'll see how muting technique works in a musical context in some upcoming examples, but before we do, let's get our muting muscles warmed up.

"I often warm up with something like this [*plays Ex. 1*]," says Bortnick. "My picking hand

HEAVY HITTERS

With funk—as with any style of music—one of the best ways to develop your craft is to transcribe parts off records and figure out what your favorite players are up to. "Even without transcribing," says Avi Bortnick, "it's important to listen to records that feature funky rhythm guitar. That helps you internalize the sounds, the common voicings and riff vocabulary, the rhythmic feel, and so on."

So who should you listen to? "It's pointless to try to say who's the 'best,'" says Bortnick. "There are so many great players and several different strains of funk." Still, you've got to start someplace, and Bortnick is happy to offer his personal essential-listening list:

• **Nile Rodgers** "Rodgers' flawless rhythm playing gave an immediately identifiable bounce to Chic hits of the 1970s and early '80s. Most well-known is 'Le Freak,' on which he employed triads, single-note lines, and double-stops. His feel and direct-to-the-board tone on 'Le Freak' are elusive—as evidenced by the difficulty most cover-band guitarists have at truly capturing the supreme groovaciousness of the original track."

• **Al McKay** "Earth, Wind & Fire's super-happening Al McKay helped set the standard for what guitar could mean for the groove of a tune. Check out how seamlessly his part locks with the percussion on 'Getaway' [from *Spirit*]. He was also masterful at creating dual-guitar funk grooves, as heard on the intro to 'Shining Star' [*That's the Way of the World*]."

• **Tony Maiden and Al Ciner** "With his deep-in-the-pocket rhythms, Tony Maiden had an inspired freedom and

is just going up and down in a 16th-note rhythm, and my other hand is squeezing a chord every 16th-note. That helps develop the relationship between your fretting-hand thumb and fingers—that pressing-on-and-off action. This isn't the most musical exercise—you could do the same thing with triads or small chords, if you like, or even a simple Caribbean groove like this [*plays Ex. 2*], which features muted 'scratches' on beats *one, two, three,* and *four.*"

Ex. 1

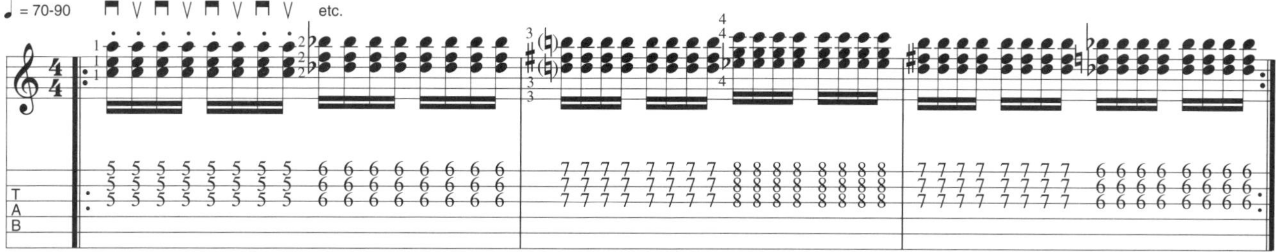

Ex. 2

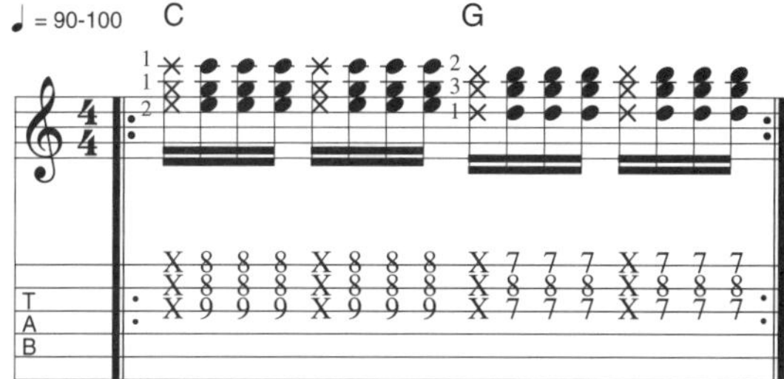

spirit in his playing. Check out his super-funky single-note grooves on the intro and choruses of Rufus's 'Dance Wit Me' [from *Rufus Featuring Chaka Khan*] and how he combines single-note lines and dominant-7th chords in the verses. Also outstanding is Maiden's work on 'Once You Get Started' [*Rufusized*].

"Al Ciner was another excellent Rufus guitarist—he appeared on their first records. Standout tracks include 'Tell Me Something Good' and 'You Got the Love' [*Rags to Rufus*], which has a relentless groove featuring skanky, bent double-stops."

• **Prince** "'Lady Cab Driver' from *1999* is one track I like a lot—though anytime Prince plays rhythm, it's a glorious experience. He has also had some very funky guitarists in his bands over the years—including Wendy Melvoin, Miko, and Levi Seacer, Jr."

• **Bo Diddley** "You don't know how happening the Bo Diddley beat is until you check out how the inventor himself played it on his recordings from the 1950s, when the groove was all goosed up with amp reverb and tremolo and maracas shaking in the background. The Bo Diddley groove is the core of many funk grooves that came later."

• **Roger Troutman** "The leader of the great '70s and '80s funk band Zapp, Troutman played skin-tight, high-voiced rhythm guitar on hits such as 'More Bounce to the Ounce' [*Zapp*]. Who needs an amp when a mixing board can sound so good?"

Now that we've got the basic right- and left-hand techniques cooking, let's put them to work in some real grooves. Check out Ex. 3a, a single-note line with a *D7* flavor. (As the line has no defining major 3rd or minor 3rd, it could just as well serve as a *Dm7* phrase.) On its own it's just dandy, but we can flesh it out with scratches in Ex. 3b.

"Deciding when to play it straight or when to add scratches," says Bortnick, "is a question of what kind of vibe you're going for at the moment, what's going on around you, and how much drive you want to give the music. Do you want to take charge and drive the groove home, or just play a little part that fits in?"

Ex. 3a

Ex. 3b

Offering another example of the muting/scratching technique, Bortnick plays Ex. 4a, a two-bar cousin of Ex. 3a that fits with *A7#9*. (Note the subtle variation between the two measures—check out beat *four* in each bar.) Adds Bortnick: "In something like this [*plays Ex. 4b*], all the funk is in the fretting hand. If I played the same thing and left my hand off the neck, I'd just be strumming away, with four or five open strings going *jang-a-lang-a-lang-a.*"

Ex. 4a

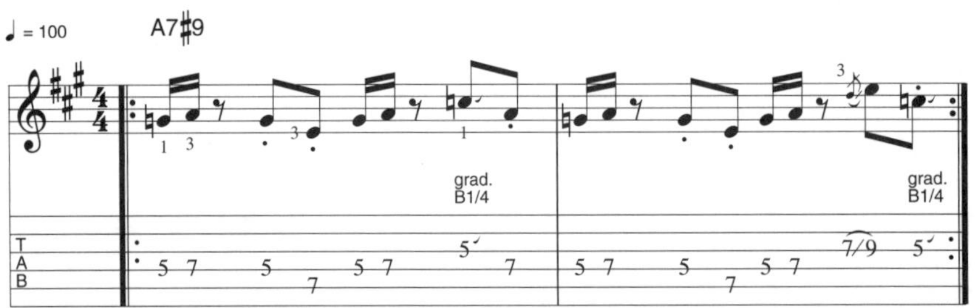

Ex. 4b

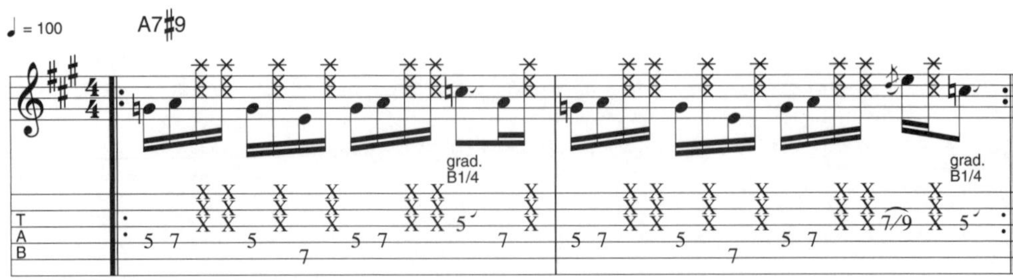

"When you distill things down to the basics," says Bortnick, "you find a lot of funk rhythms come out of the Afro-Cuban clave rhythm most of us know as the Bo Diddley beat.' Check this elementary one-bar *Em7* rhythm pattern [*plays Ex. 5a*]."

Ex. 5a

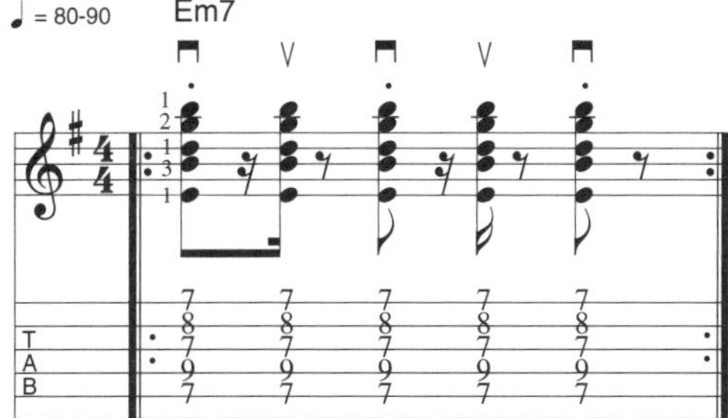

Even though Ex. 5a's rhythm is somewhat sparse, your picking hand should be moving up and down at a 16th-note clip. This helps keep your groove rock-solid. Simply move your picking hand ever-so-slightly away from the strings when you don't want them to sound. The upstroke and downstroke indications should help clarify matters. As with Examples 3a and 4a, you can dress up Ex. 5a with scratches, as illustrated in Ex. 5b.

Ex. 5b

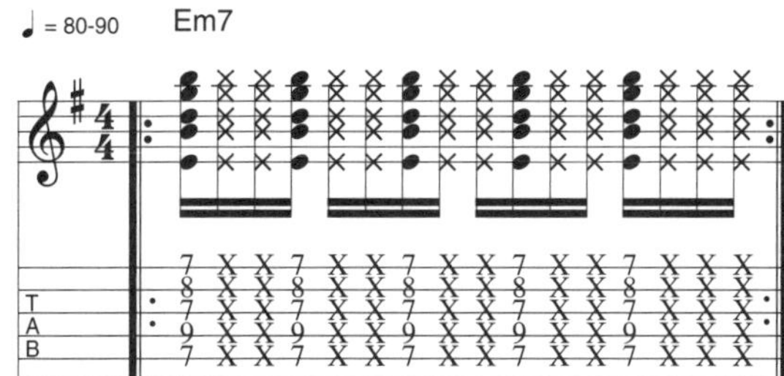

"You can take that basic phrase," Bortnick says, "and move it over one 16th-note to get this cool variation [*plays Ex. 5c*]. And you can move it over another 16th—now an eighth-note later than Ex. 5a—to get this [*plays Ex. 5d*], and so on. Each variation is equally funky. Deciding which variation to use depends on how you want to interact with the bass line. You can accent the same beats, or play something that bounces off the bass line—something that fills in the holes, or 'answers' it.

"If you displace the start of our original phrase [Ex. 5a] far enough, eventually the two halves of the bar switch places, giving you this [*plays Ex. 5e*]—which feels pretty different. In Afro-Cuban circles they'd call that a '2–3 clave' because there are two attacks in the first half of the rhythm and three in the second half. In contrast, our starting figure would be considered a '3–2 clave.' Though funk is not nearly as codified as Afro-Cuban music, there is a lot of overlap, and the 3–2/2–3 concept is a neat distinction that can help you understand different types of funk rhythms."

Ex. 5c

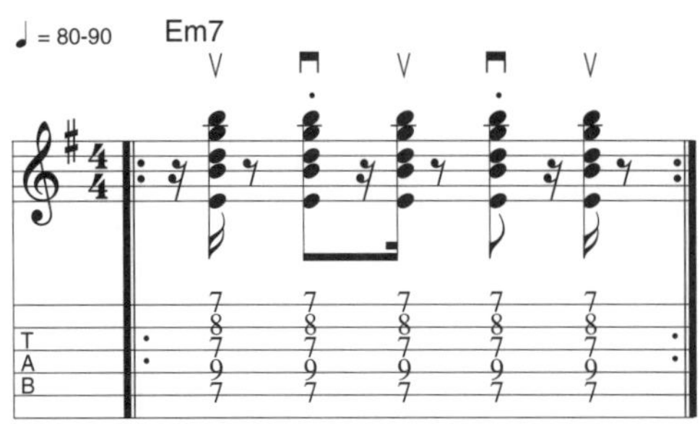

Ex. 5d

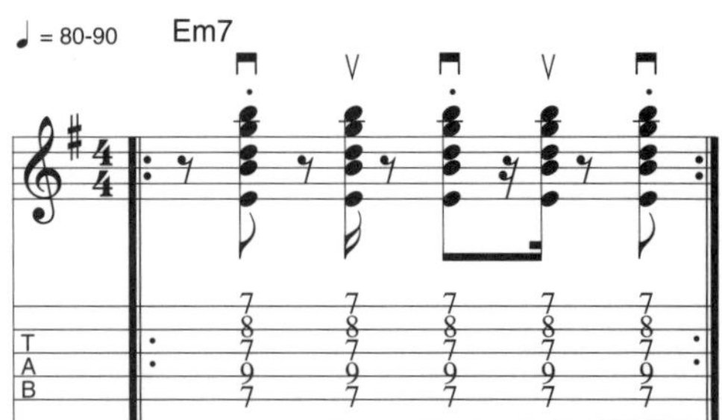

Ex. 5e

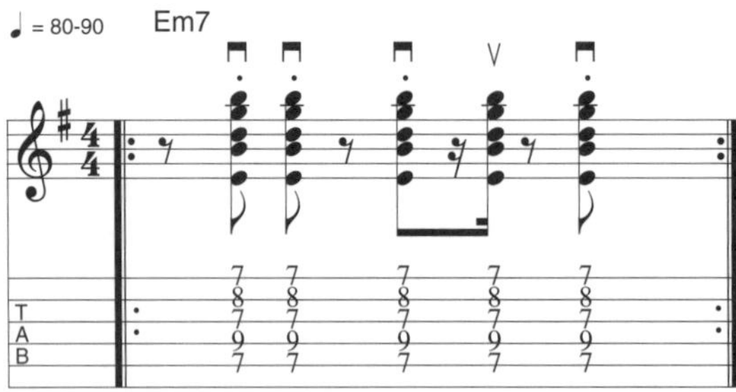

"Dorian harmonies are very common in funk," says Bortnick, "so they're worth getting to know. Something like this [*plays Ex. 6a*] is a standard Dorian-based riff you might play over a *Bm7–E9* vamp. You could even superimpose this figure over a static *Bm7* vamp—or when you just have *E9*—to add some subtle harmonic movement."

Ex. 6a

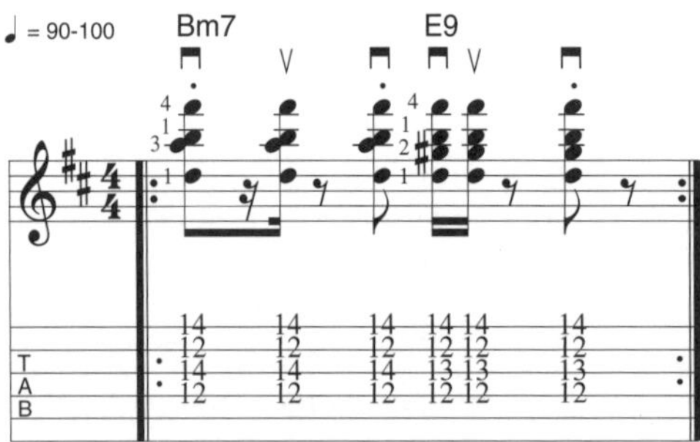

What makes a progression Dorian? If we take the two chords involved—*Bm7* (*B–D–F#–A*) and *E9* (*E–G#–B–D-F#*)—and string together the tones of both chords, we get *B, D, E, F#, G#, A*. With just six degrees, that's an incomplete scale, but it looks more like *B* Dorian (*B, C#, D, E, F#, G#, A*) than any other common *B*-minor scale or mode. (Note the relationship of the chords: Im7–IV7. Any time you see a progression like this, it's safe to assume Dorian.)

Ex. 6b offers several pairs of alternate voicing—all of which can be plugged into Ex. 6a's rhythmic formula. The final pair is actually a single chord form that can stand in for *Bm11* or *E9*. Example 6c—in the style of Prince's "Kiss" riff—shows the voicing in action.

Ex. 6b

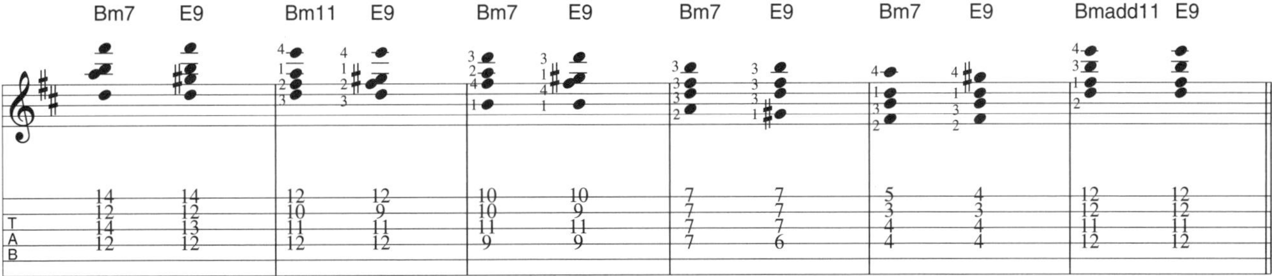

Ex. 6c

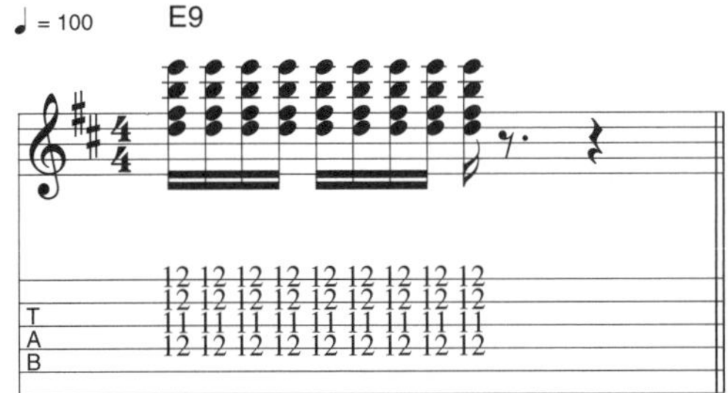

Now that our funk muscles are getting stronger, it's time to stretch into more adventurous rhythmic territory. Example 7a is a two-bar funk phrase based on *D7* and incorporating 9 and ♯9 colors. "Even though the chord's flavor changes as the top note moves," says Bortnick, "I think of this as basically a one-chord vamp." Example 7b is a greasy variation on Ex. 7a's first bar, with a chordal slide on beat *one*.

Ex. 7a

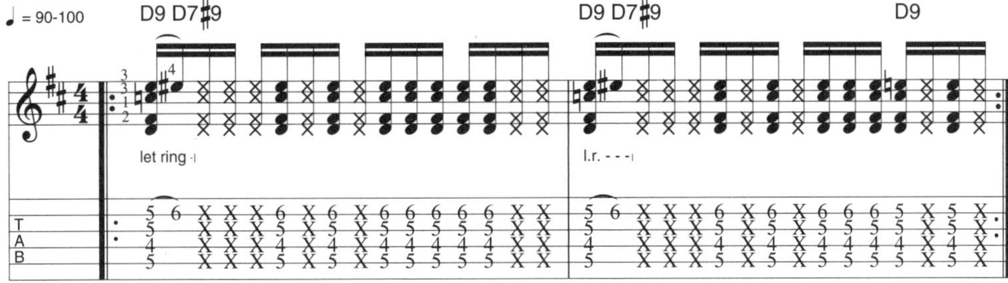

Ex. 7b

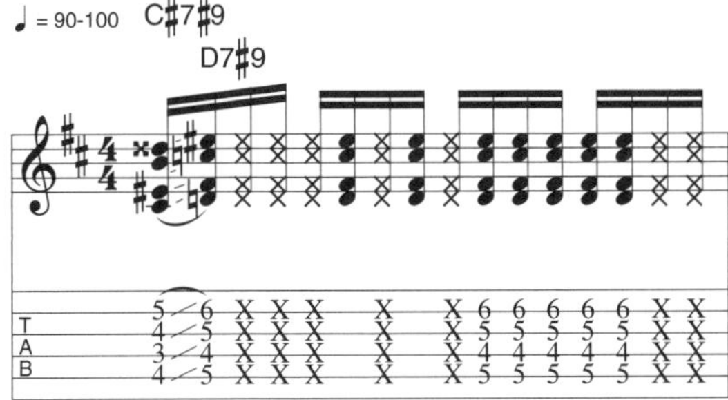

Though funk rhythm guitar is more about rhythmic repetition than variety (the aim is to create a danceable, hypnotic groove—not to impress drummers with how many hip syncopations you can squeeze out of a chord), there's usually some room for an occasional fill or turnaround at the end of a phrase. Example 7c shows how Ex. 7a could be tweaked to add a little harmonic and rhythmic spice.

Ex. 7c

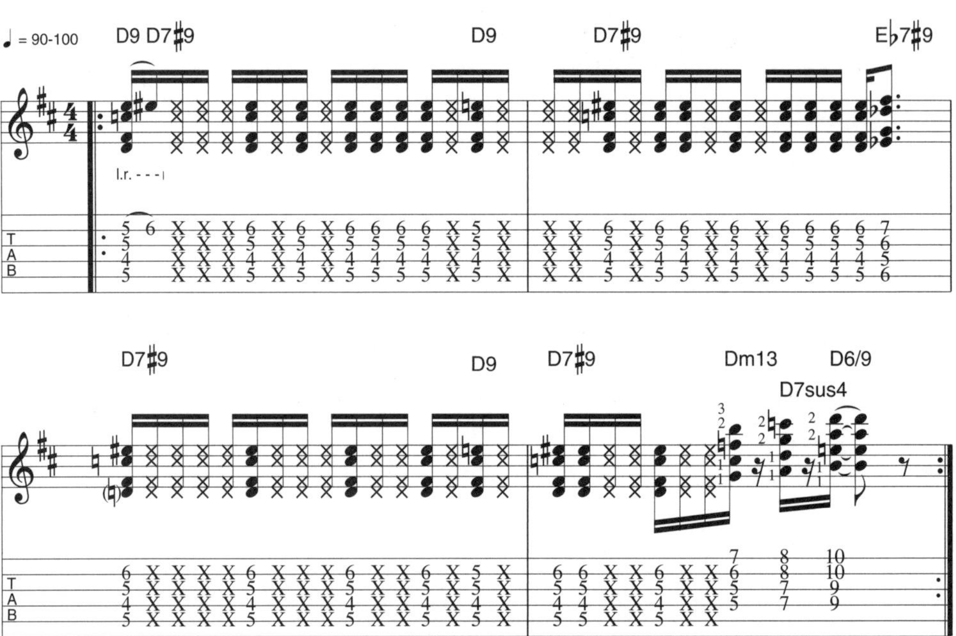

Examples 7d and 7e—either of which could supplant Ex. 7c's bar 4—offer even more options. "Both fills start with descending triads that I 'borrowed' from [keyboardist] Billy Preston's signature riff on 'Will It Go Round in Circles,'" notes Bortnick. Example 7d is the skankier of the two—with beats *three* and *four* suggesting the style of Rufus guitarist Al Ciner. Example 7e is closer to Preston's vibey original.

Ex. 7d

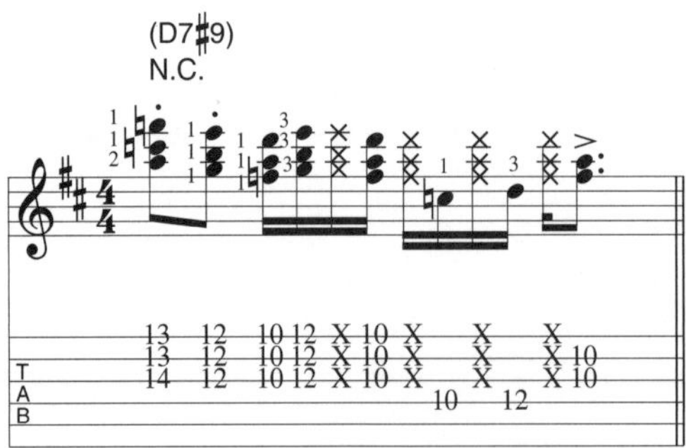

Ex. 7e

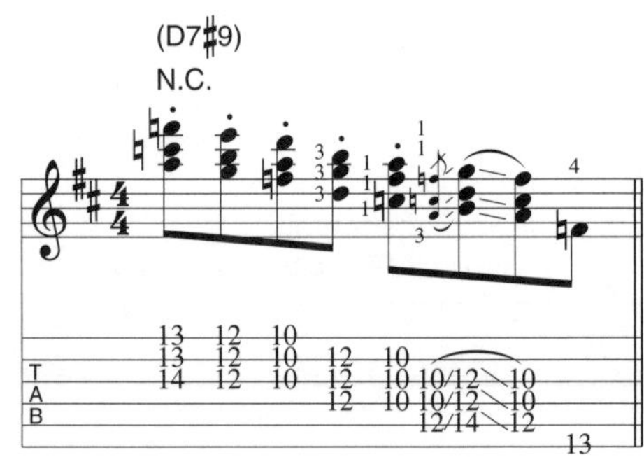

TEACHING AN OLD WAH NEW TRICKS

While you can get plenty funky without one, a wah-wah pedal can come in handy when it's time to get down. But before you bolt that Crybaby or Vox wah onto your pedalboard, beware—using any mass-produced pedal in a conventional way can easily make you sound like every other guitarist on the block. But Bortnick assures us there are ways to work a wah into your groove without explicitly referencing the blaxploitation films of the '70s.

"Most players use wahs in time with the music," says Bortnick, "going down-up-down-up in time with the eighth-notes. That's *wacka-ohka-wacka-ohka* if you're strumming 16ths. That's cool, but it can get corny. An alternate approach would be to work the pedal up and down in a half-note rhythm—down for two beats and up for two: *wacka-wacka-wacka-wacka-ohka-ohka-ohka-ohka.* But the wah is just a filter, and there's no reason you have to use it in time with the music. You can step on it just to accent certain parts of a groove—to give bass notes more bass and high parts more bite. Another option is to make long, slow filter sweeps, raising and lowering the pedal over the course of two or three measures—that's the kind of thing you sometimes hear in techno music. You can even leave it parked in one position—halfway down for a pinched sound or pedal-to-the-metal for a real skanky tone. By using wah creatively, you can avoid the obvious retro clichés."

This cache of riffs should give you plenty of food for funk thought. If you want to keep the disco ball rolling, here are a few final words of funk wisdom from our guide:

- "There's a huge tonal difference between playing hard with your volume rolled back a little or playing gently with your volume wide open. As I may play any given passage harder or softer for timbral reasons, I'm always adjusting my Strat's volume knob to keep the overall volume about the same."
- "Experiment with effects, including tried-and-true funk tools such as wah-wah, envelope filter (auto-wah), phaser, and delay. Each of these has many uses, from cliché to novel."
- "You must have solid rhythm to play funk. One thing I've done to practice rhythm is to program a drum machine so that it randomly drops some beats rather than beating the time into your head. That helps you develop your internal clock."
- "Play with musicians who have a solid, funky time feel, especially bassists and drummers."
- "One mistake jazz players make when they play funk is that they swing the 16th notes. That can be cool when you're doing it intentionally for a certain kind of groove, but make sure you're conscious of the difference between swing 16ths and straight 16ths."
- "Sometimes the little sparse part can be nastier and funkier than the overt, full-on rhythm-machine thing."
- "If you're playing something that makes you want to move, then you're probably doing it right."

ROCK: FROM ANARCHY TO ANACHRONISM IN 20 EASY RIFFS

How Yesterday's Rhythm Radicals Became Today's Retro-Rockers

BY JOE GORE

Johnny Marr

The post-punk guitarist of 15 years ago wanted to kill Jimmy Page; today's alternative rocker wants to be him.

That's a gross oversimplification, but the rhythm guitar riffs compiled here document the transition from a generation of players who wanted to throw out everything that had come before to one that gleefully embraces earlier styles with varying degrees of irony.

While it's sometimes hard to see connections between the bad-attitude provocateurs of the late '70s and the current stadium rockers we refer to—with straight faces—as "alternative," there *are* common threads between the players who once opposed the mainstream and those who currently help define it. Perhaps the key trait that unites them is an intuitive distrust of polish, a shared notion that music's emotional context takes precedence over the niceties of its construction. In other words, attitude outweighs execution.

For all their piss and vinegar, the Class of '77 punk guitarists offered few new sounds; their second-hand primitivism was largely derived from rockabilly, instrumental rock, and the '60s garage school. But by the end of the decade, Ramones-style power-chording and Chuck Berry-on-smack solos were increasingly supplanted by more radical textures.

Sex Pistol Johnny Rotten resurfaced as John Lydon fronting P.I.L., whose revolutionary instrumental style spanned rock, dub, and *musique concrète* experimentation. Keith Levene's rhythm riff from the band's first single, "Public Image," casts a long shadow over the '80s. In Ex. 1, the harmonically ambiguous ostinato double-stops over a I–V bass line in straight eighth-notes foreshadows U2, the Psychedelic Furs, and countless other bands. Edge and Andy Summers both relied heavily on the technique of setting a one- or two-note figure against a shifting chord progression implied by the bass.

Ex. 1

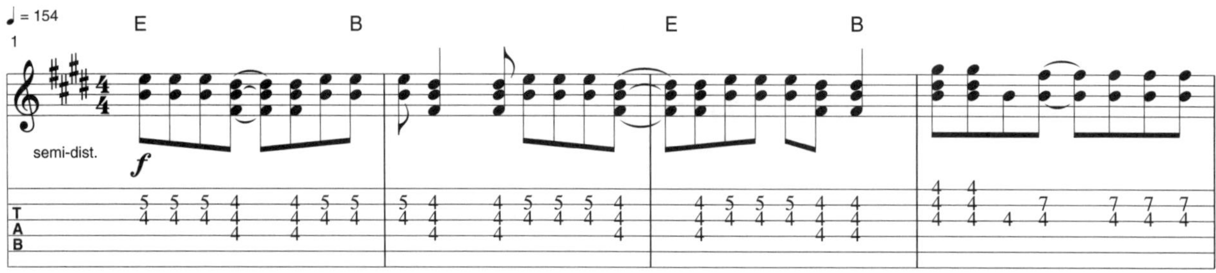

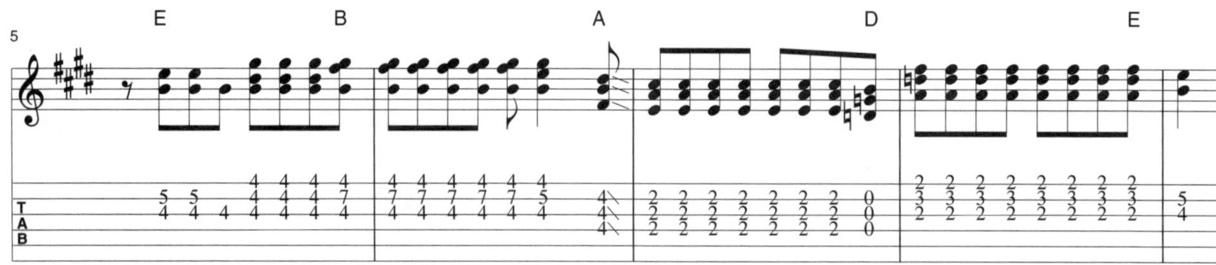

Colin Newman and Bruce Gilbert of the abstract-minimalist band Wire favored metronomic rhythms, deadpan delivery, and uncompromisingly grating textures on tunes like "Two People in a Room" (Ex. 2). Use heavy downstrokes for maximum ouch.

Gang of Four's Andy Gill was perhaps the most radical player of the immediate post-punk era. With his harsh, solid-state-distortion tone and a stabbing rhythmic style that can only be described as spastic, he sounded like no one else before or since. Example 3 shows the sort of asymmetrical accents he unleashed on the intro to "At Home He's a Tourist."

Ex. 2

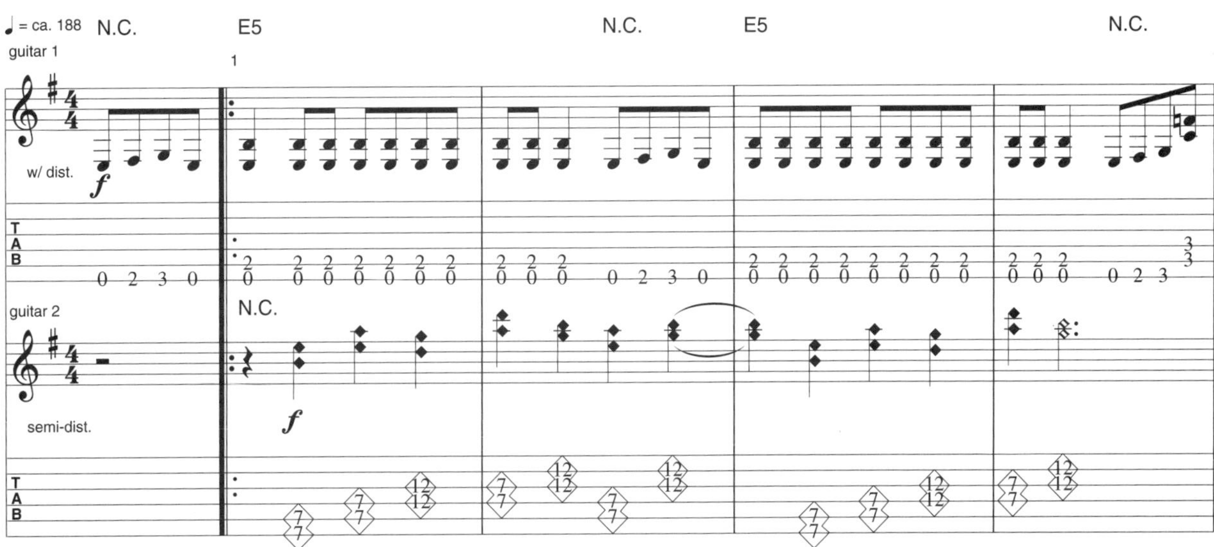
♩ = ca. 188
N.C.
E5
N.C.
E5
N.C.
guitar 1
w/ dist.
guitar 2
N.C.
semi-dist.

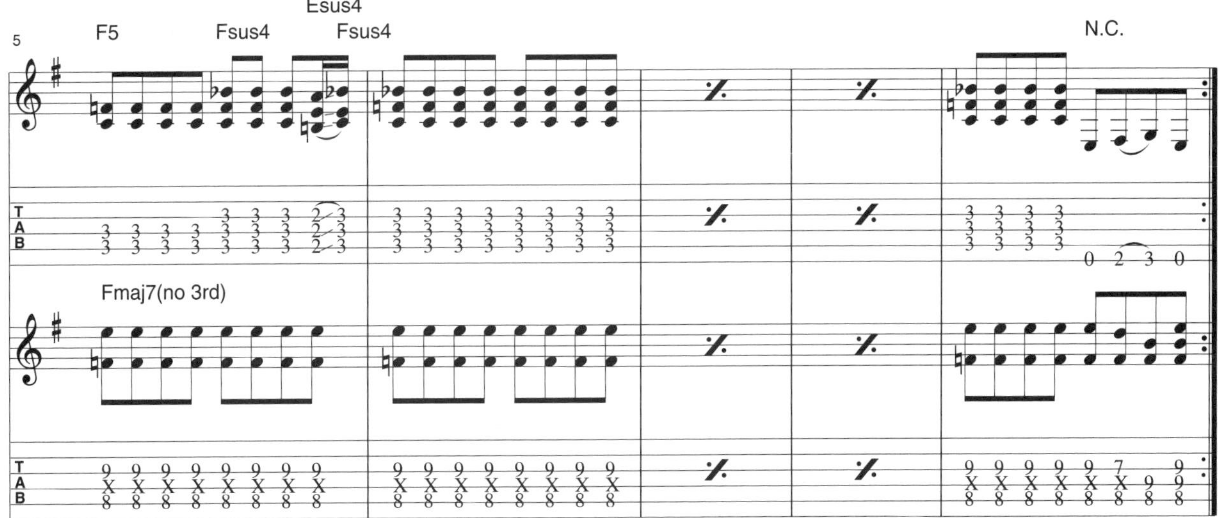
F5
Fsus4
Esus4
Fsus4
N.C.
Fmaj7(no 3rd)

Ex. 3

During his tenure with Bauhaus, Daniel Ash often bypassed chordal playing in favor of heavily effected, dubbed-out noises over simple, repetitive bass lines. Check Examples 4a and 4b, which recall the intro to "Stigmata Martyr." Like his fellow design-conscious proto-Goth—the Cure's Robert Smith—Ash made ingenious use of echo and delay effects, helping inspire a new interest in atmospheric texture. Ash also packs a mean EBow sustainer.

Ex. 4a

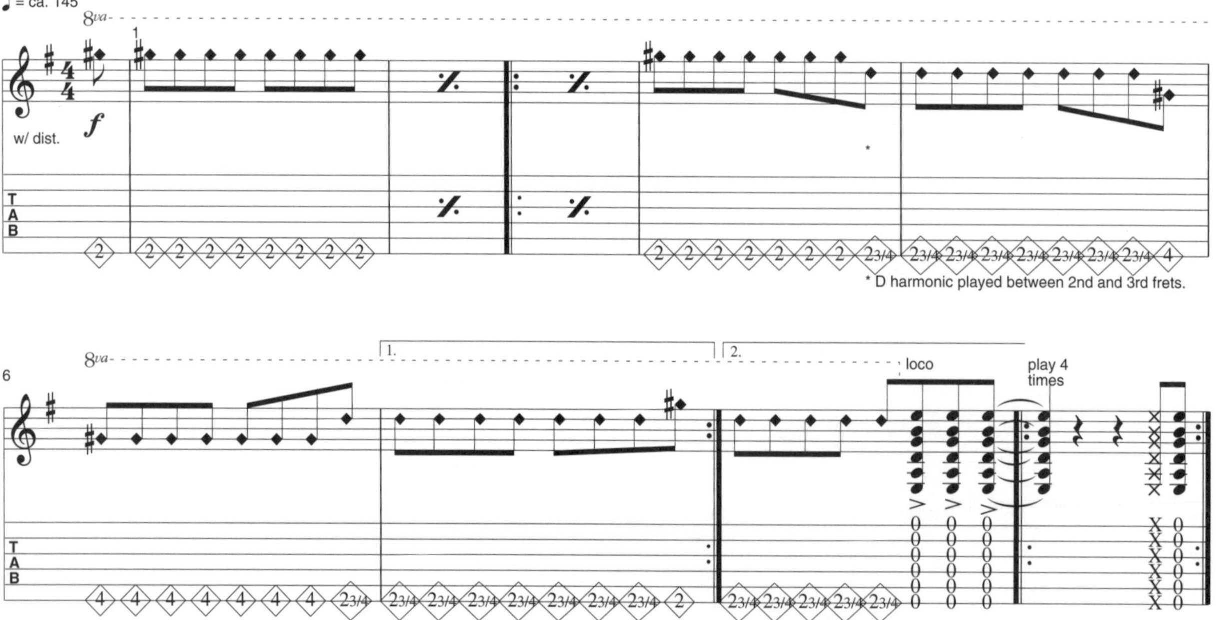

Ex. 4b

Off-kilter popsters Andy Partridge and Dave Gregory of XTC paired Beatlesque melodies with clanging, *outré* guitars, as in the main riff from *Black Sea*'s "Respectable Street." In Ex. 5, note how simply sliding an open-position *C* chord up a fret yields something completely different.

Ex. 5

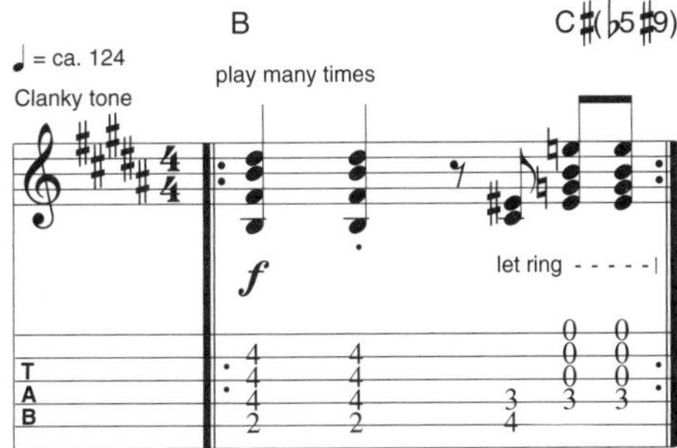

England's multiracial "Two-Tone" ska scene fused post-punk energy with Afro-Caribbean rhythms. Similarly, American avant-funk artists like Prince and Defunkt helped dismantle the musical apartheid that had arisen during the disco era. Early Prince grooves like Ex. 6 set brittle, clipped syncopations against rock-simple eighth-note drum grooves.

Ex. 6

Meanwhile, early-'80s Talking Heads borrowed heavily from the two-guitar rhythm grooves of Nigeria's Fela Kuti, who borrowed heavily from the grooves of James Brown, who sounded quite African in the first place. The third guitar part in the "I Zimbra" groove [from *Fear of Music*] evokes traditional West African bell patterns; Ex. 7 illustrates the style.

Ex. 7

A similar groove consciousness helped define L.A.'s alternative sounds, percolating through the music of Fishbone, the Chili Peppers, and Jane's Addiction's funkier moments, like the wicked feel from "Been Caught Stealing," which Dave Navarro played in part on a miked, unplugged electric (Ex. 8).

Ex. 8

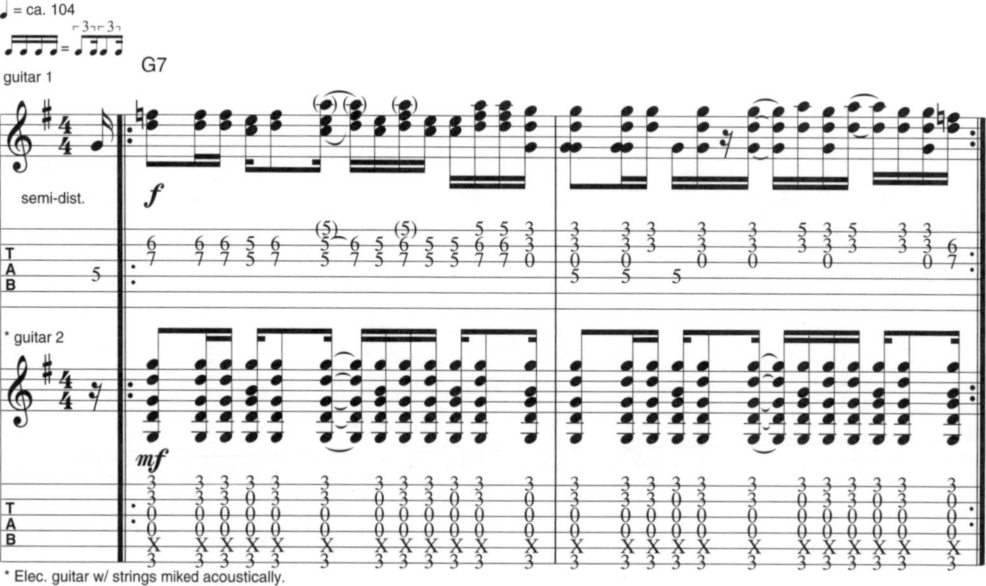

* Elec. guitar w/ strings miked acoustically.

Cocteau Twin Robin Guthrie coated simple parts with a thick shellac of signal processing, creating lush, unabashedly pretty textures and inaugurating the "dream pop" genre. Example 9 shows a *DADGAD*-tuned figure—typical of his ultra-idiomatic fingerings—from songs like "Millimillenary."

Ex. 9

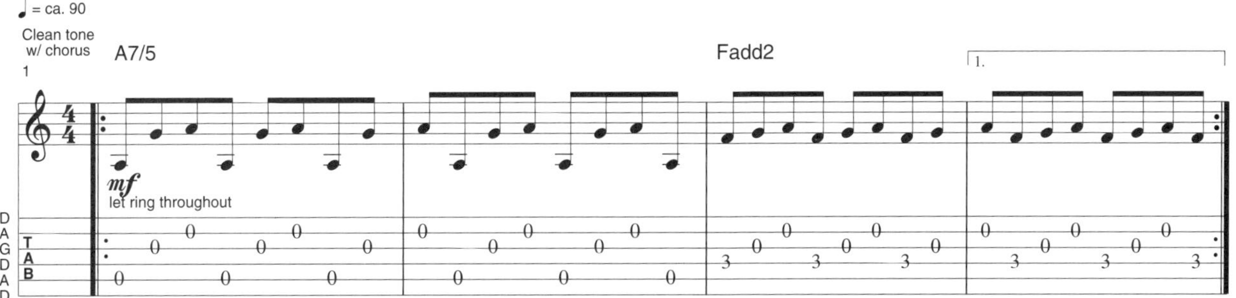

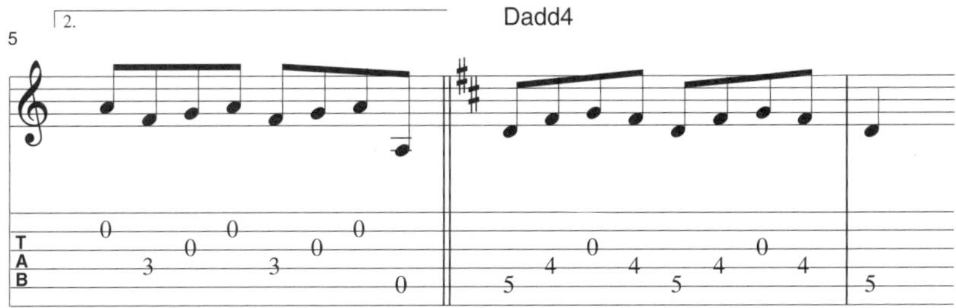

Inspired by the procedures of electric guitar composers Rhys Chatham and Glenn Branca, Sonic Youth used volume and dozens of new tunings to create guitar colors unprecedented in rock. Many of their tunings, including the *G*-major pentatonic configuration Thurston Moore uses for the main riff from "Teenage Riot," feature smaller-than-normal intervals between strings. Sonic Youth's guitars are often restrung with gauges corresponding to normal *A*, *D*, and *G* strings; Ex. 10 uses only *G* and *D* strings.

Later on, My Bloody Valentine mastermind Kevin Shields crafted bold, otherworldly textures via elaborate signal processing, psychoactive whammy-bar manipulation, dense overdubs, and sequenced samples of his own guitar noises. Example 11 shows how Shields fit melodies from tunes like "I Only Said"—a bit of sampled feedback, played on a keyboard and detuned with the pitch wheel—over a sparsely voiced and whammy-bar-spiced rhythm part.

The Smiths may have talked a lot about returning to unpretentious pop values, but there was little tradition in Johnny Marr's relentlessly inventive playing beyond his unerring knack for crafting great pop hooks. Tunes like "This Charming Man," the group's first big single, featured an inspired mix of African highlife, neo-'60s jangle-pop, and Marr's uniquely zingy melodicism (Ex. 12).

Ex. 10

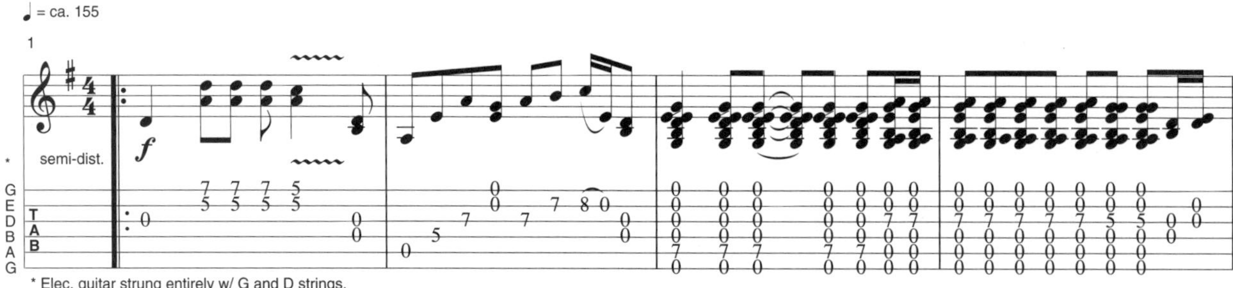
♩ = ca. 155
semi-dist.
* Elec. guitar strung entirely w/ G and D strings.

Ex. 11

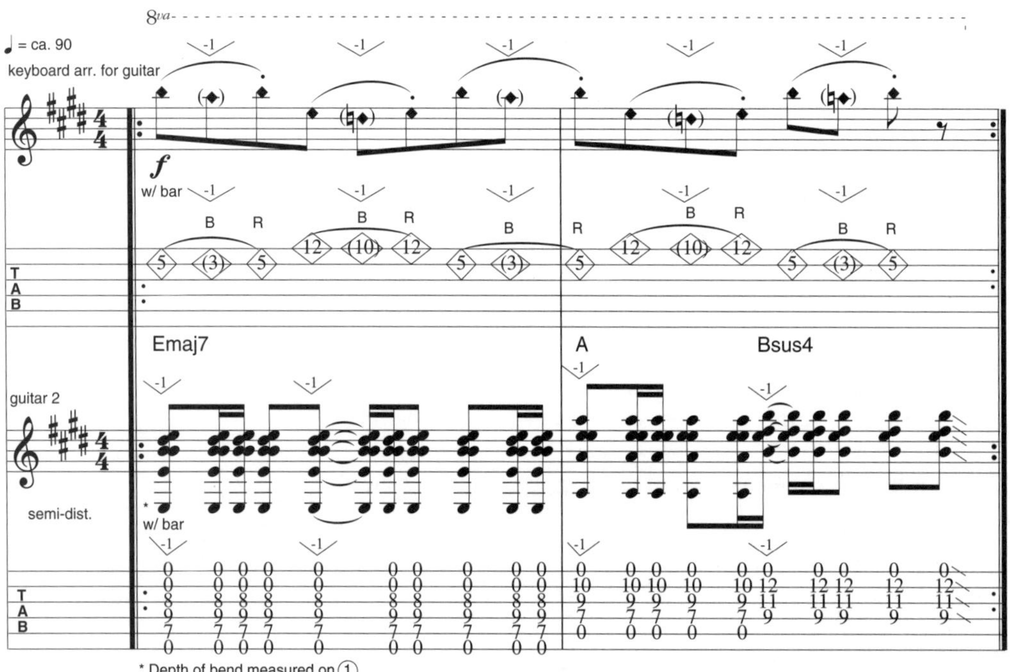
♩ = ca. 90
keyboard arr. for guitar
8va
w/ bar
Emaj7
A
Bsus4
guitar 2
semi-dist.
* Depth of bend measured on ①.

Ex. 12

♩ = ca. 208
*Tune up 1/2 step (F B♭ E♭ A♭ C F)
Solo guitar

*All notes sound 1/2 step higher than written.

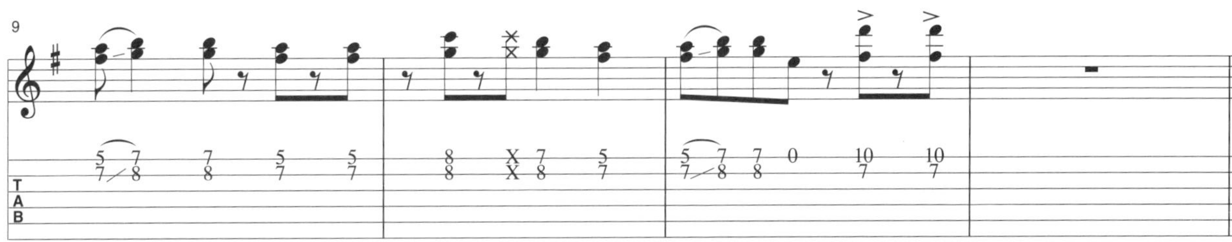

While iconoclasts like Sonic Youth and Kevin Shields were creating entirely new sounds, once-discredited '70s rock sounds and attitudes were gradually becoming fashionable again. Intellectually upscale post-punk bands were growing more metallic as metal became punkier. The Scorpions and the Sex Pistols were universes apart; not so Metallica and Killing Joke, whose guitarist, Geordie, specialized in muscular, distorted riffs like the one from "Age of Greed" (Ex. 13).

Ex. 13

♩ = ca. 158
⑥ = D

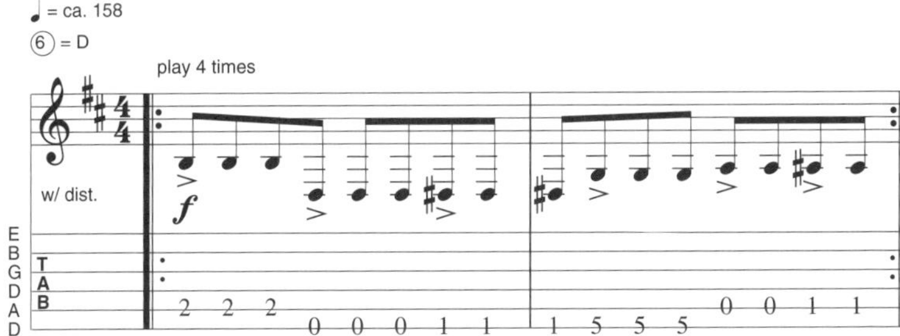

The great wall between punk and metal was falling, and James Hetfield's summation of how early Metallica differed from some of their contemporaries ("We were all energy and no posing") applies just as readily to the proto-grunge of Seattle's Melvins and Green River. Soundgarden was positively Sabbathesque from the get-go, as on this early riff (Ex. 14).

Ex. 14

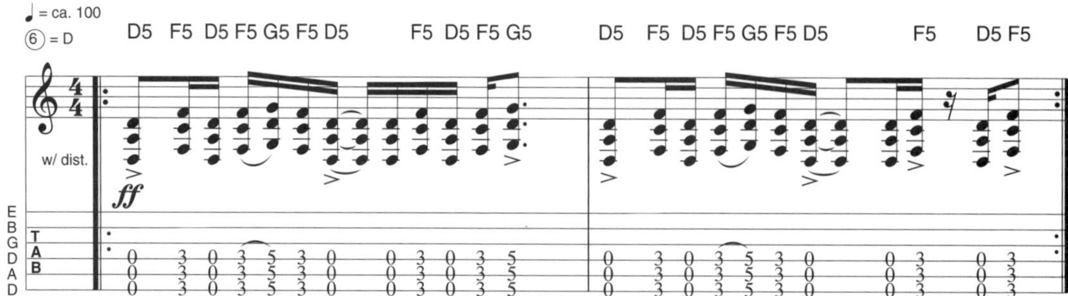

The return to the 6-string values of the '70s hardly stops with over-the-top metal. When Neil Young wrote a song about Johnny Rotten in 1979, Lydon repaid the favor by calling Young a "whiny old hippie." But today Neil is rightly hailed as the Godfather of Grunge. You can certainly hear it in the open-position rave-ups of Dinosaur Jr.'s J Mascis (Ex. 15). The metallic and folk-punk strains converged in Nirvana (Ex. 16).

Ex. 15

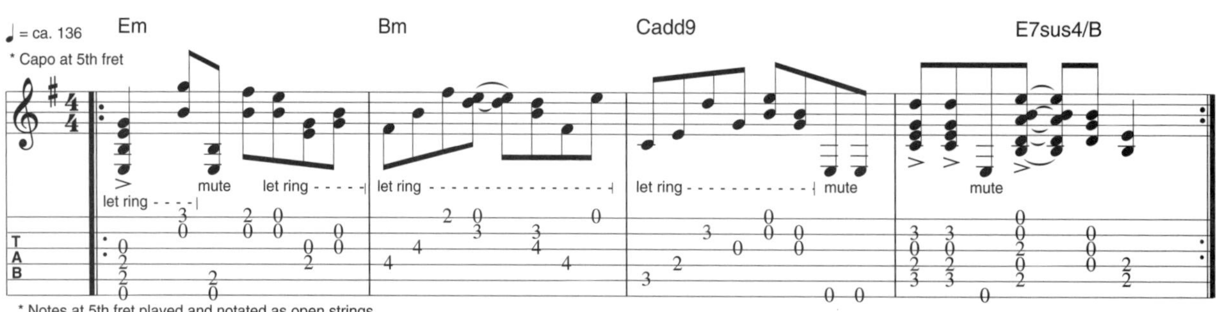

* Notes at 5th fret played and notated as open strings.

Ex. 16

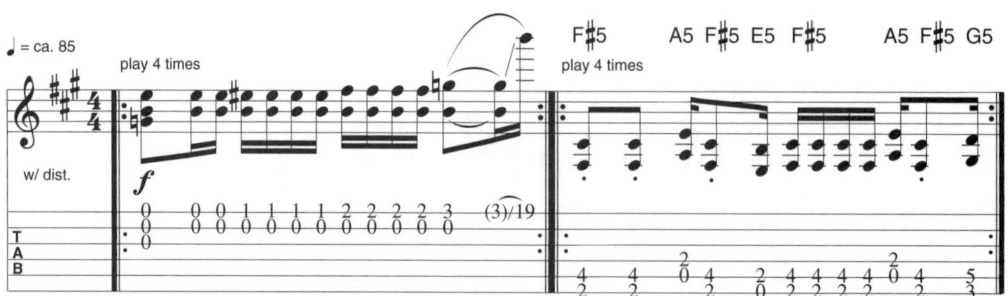

Today the testosterone-fueled riff reigns supreme. From the industrial/metal crossover of Nine Inch Nails and Ministry to the hammer-headed "smart metal" of Rage Against the Machine and Helmet, florid solos are out in favor of the sort of cyber-Sabbath power chording heard in Ex. 17's Helmet-type riff.

Ex. 17

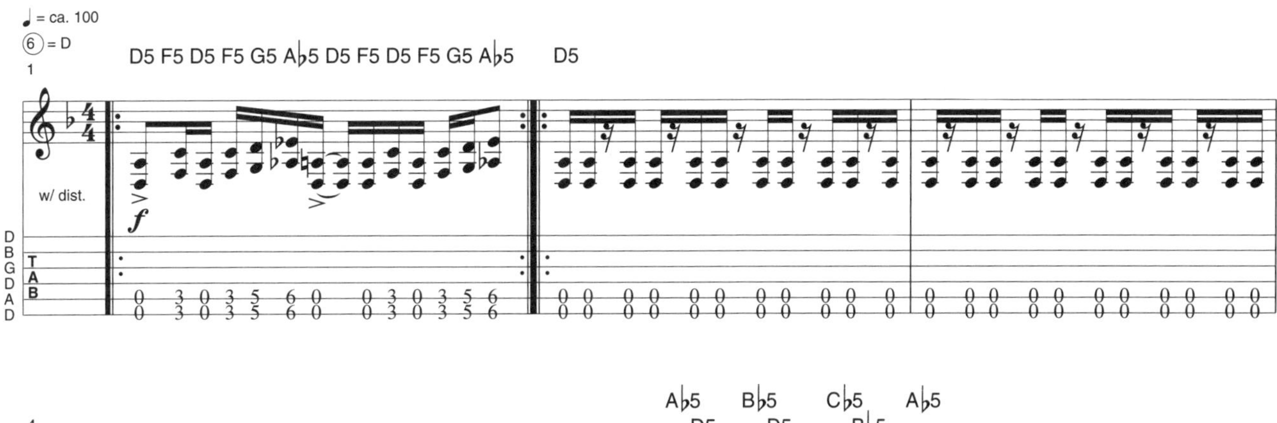

REGGAE: JAMAICAN GROOVES

Smoke Up the House with These Burning Riddims

Bob Marley

BY ANDY BASSFORD

The basic reggae rhythm pattern is called the *ska* (rhymes with *yeah,* not *Jah*). The word also refers to a dance and a jazzy pre-reggae Jamaican music that first appeared in the early '60s. The ska rhythm in Ex. 1 became integral to the rock-steady style that succeeded ska in the mid '60s and has been the backbone of Jamaican reggae to this day. The ska is generally played by guitar and piano in unison.

For an authentic sound, use barre chords between the 1st and 10th frets. Strum through all the strings, emphasizing the highest ones. (Some players use only the top four strings.) Swing the right hand freely without muting. A quick, consistent left-hand release is essential. The ska should be about the same duration as a hand-clap, yet every note of the chord should be distinct. Occasionally the ska is sustained a bit longer, depending on how the pianist is playing. Use a fairly light touch and make sure your inversions complement the keyboard parts. Some reggae tunes call for a behind-the-beat feel, while others are more on the beat. Your amp should be set clean and not too loud, with plenty of presence and treble.

Ex. 1

In the late '60s the pattern in Ex. 2 became popular. It's possible this rhythm grew from an attempt to manually imitate the sound of an electronic delay. Jamaican musicians call this the "double riff," "double stroke," or *checkae* (that's how the rhythm sounds). Mute the strings with the left hand after playing a ska and catch the high strings on the upstroke. This rhythm has either a straight-eighth or shuffle feel, depending on what the hi-hat and organ left hand are playing. You often find a swing feel at slower tempos.

Around this time the music began to be called reggae, a word that has come to stand for all Jamaican roots music. The pattern in Ex. 2 is what many people think of as *the* reggae rhythm, due to its currency in the '70s, when the music of Bob Marley, Toots & the Maytals, and Burning Spear became widely known in the U.S.

Ex. 2

The pattern in Ex. 3 was also popular around the same time. It is derived from mento, a pre-ska folk style, but the accents are different in reggae mento. It is basically a double riff with an added upstroke. Of the three 16th-notes, the first upstroke is held longest; the downstroke is accented but held shortest. Traditional mento strums are much more even. At very slow tempos this pattern can be played with all downstrokes.

Ex. 3

In the mid '70s, the basic drum style changed (Ex. 4), and tempos slowed drastically as a result. Although the double riff was occasionally heard on sessions, players started to go back to the straight ska because it was too hard to sync up the double riff with the new, busier hi-hat patterns.

Ex. 4

Toward the end of the '70s the drum style changed again and began to resemble slow funk and rock grooves. The tempo came back up, making room for a new semi-mento style (Ex. 5). Sometimes one guitar would play this pattern while the other played the ska, but more often this part showed up in a variation of the ska, as in Ex. 6. At faster tempos, you may find it easier to play the last two strums in this pattern as upstrokes.

Ex. 5

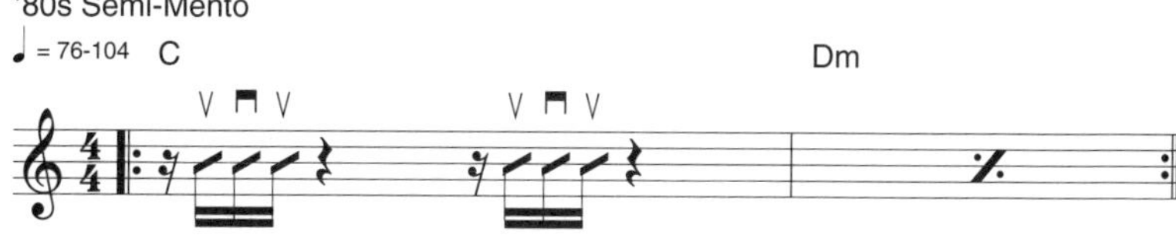

Ex. 6

Guitarists also experimented with changing the inversions of the basic chords while playing this rhythm, giving the part a melodic function (Ex. 7)—again, at faster tempos you might play this with all upstrokes. In the late '80s the advent of dancehall reggae, with its complex drum machine patterns and much faster tempos, resulted in guitarists abandoning these variations and returning to the straight ska.

Ex. 7

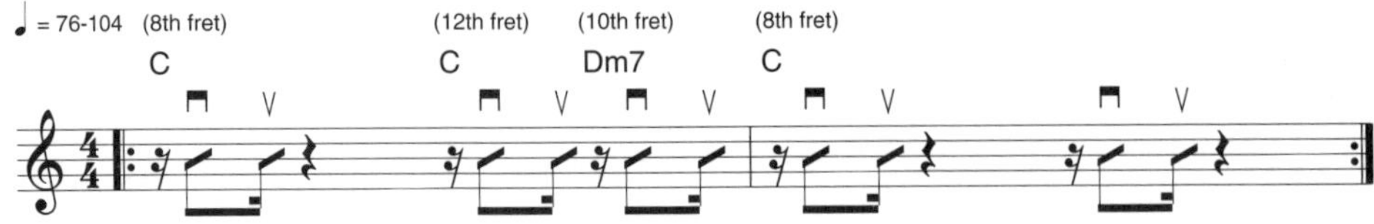

In many of today's Jamaican sessions, the ska is played with one-hand synth chords and rhythm guitar is ignored altogether. When a guitar appears, it often plays a lead pattern and is used as a flavoring rather than a staple. However, contemporary reggae bands usually include at least one guitar for live shows.

Reggae players take rhythm guitar very seriously. In fact, the lead player might more properly be called the second guitarist: If there is only one guitar on a reggae record, it is almost always rhythm. When I started doing sessions in Jamaica, I was allowed to play rhythm only if the other guitarist didn't show up! Let's explore some of the roles that the lead—ah, second—guitarist plays.

The reggae lead player works hand-in-glove with the bassist. In terms of holding down a reggae groove, the bass player has the most important gig. Bass is the foundation; classic reggae "riddims" (chord patterns and bass lines used over and over again under different melodies or raps) are identified by the bass line. The lead player's job is to enhance the bass part.

Typically, the reggae lead guitarist doubles the bass line an octave higher, adding weight and emphasis to the essential bass line. Reggae evolved under primitive conditions: Doubling the bass ensured that the line would be heard no matter how bad the recording or listening environment.

Doubling works best when the bass is playing a simple, repetitive part. To get the correct sound and feel, use a bright, clean tone (not loud!) and mute with your right hand at the bridge. To minimize intonation problems, finger the line as close to the nut as possible. Fret lightly with your left hand while still producing a clear tone, and copy the bassist's duration and accenting. The key is to be absolutely accurate and consistent with the length of each note. Watch the releases: Your left and right hands should work together to control note length. Mimicking the bass player's fingering may help match the phrasing, but if the line climbs onto the *G* string, it may be better to refinger the passage rather than to deal with the tonal difference between wound and unwound strings.

Usually all downstrokes work best for doubling, although sometimes a line grooves a little better with alternate picking. Ideally, the guitar and the bass will sound like one huge instrument. Examples 8a and 8b show two classic bass lines that have supported hundreds of reggae records.

A common variation on bass line doubling is called rolling. The guitarist uses mandolin-like trills on some notes while exactly doubling others. Examples 9a and 9b show how to roll the lines in Examples 8a and 8b—keep the left hand as light as possible. Note the harmonized notes in Ex. 9b—replacing unisons with 3rds or other intervals can add power and color if you do it with discretion.

In Ex. 10, the lead guitar plays a choppy, syncopated phrase in the spaces of the bass line. This reflects advice I got on my second session in Jamaica: "Play where the bass isn't." If the bass is playing lots of roots and 5ths, try using other chord tones. If the bass line has strong harmonic content, emphasize roots and 5ths in your guitar part.

Ex. 9a

Ex. 9b

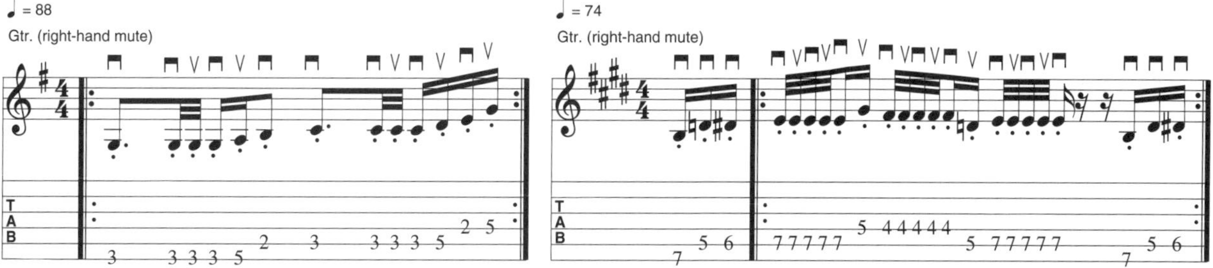

Ex. 10

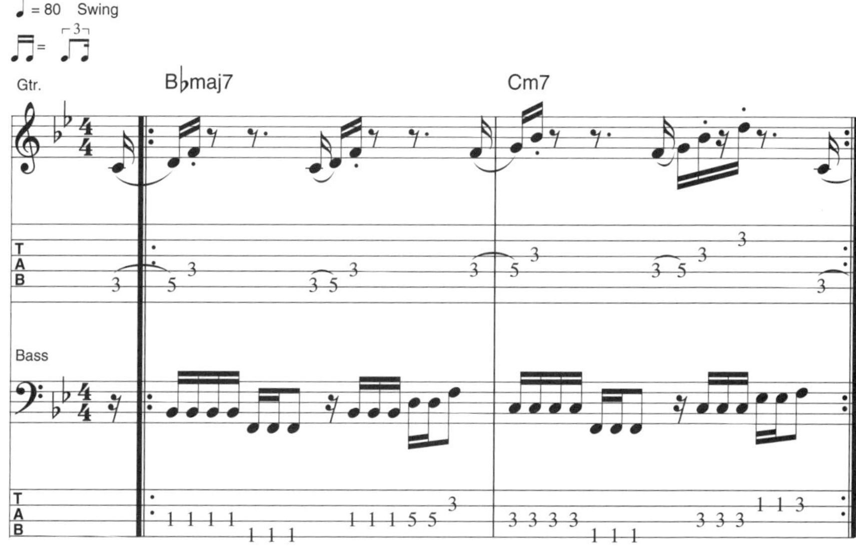

The lead part in Ex. 11 creates a running, double-time feel against the more deliberate bass part. Mute this one very, very lightly. In Ex. 12 this concept is reversed: The guitar plays a half-time, relaxed feel against the active bass line.

Many reggae tunes consist of a single bass line and a couple of chords. Sometimes the right thing to do is to lock onto one part and play it throughout the song. However, it can be effective to mix techniques, doubling the bass on the verses and playing a catchy counter-melody or counter-rhythm for the choruses, for example.

SOUL, MAN!

A Lesson with Steve Cropper

BY ANDY ELLIS

Steve Cropper, mid-'60s.

Steve Cropper may not play fast, flashy, or loud, but he's river deep. His muted, chunky lines and biting fills define soul guitar. Cropper's contributions stretch beyond his twangy Tele, however. As a member of Booker T. & the MG's, Cropper co-wrote such hits as "Green Onions" and "Time Is Tight." He also co-wrote many soul evergreens with artists like Otis Redding, Wilson Pickett, and Eddie Floyd, including "(Sittin' on) the Dock of the Bay," "In the Midnight Hour," "634-5789," and "Knock on Wood." Steve also produced the Otis Redding classics "Respect," "Shake," "Ole Man Trouble," "I've Been Loving You Too Long (to Stop Now)," and the immortal "(Sittin' on) the Dock of the Bay."

We met Steve in San Francisco—not far from that famous dock, actually—a few hours before a hot MG's reunion show. Hearing him play his timeless guitar parts in a hotel room, up front and personal, is a humbling experience.

Cropper's gift is his unerring ability to create the right part, the essential line, the killer hook. His "Soul Man" guitar groove worked magic twice: Once for Sam & Dave in '67 and then, nearly a generation later, for the gonzo Blues Brothers. This figure epitomizes Memphis soul and R&B guitar. Steve's ever-changing *doinks*, *chucks*, and rhythmic embellishments defy notation, but the cards are on the table in Ex. 1.

Ex. 1

"'Soul Man' is sort of a lick within a lick," allows Cropper, "with all those little ups and things. I play it like a drum." Strong rhythm is crucial to the big man from Memphis: "I've been a metronome all my life. If you set the groove, it *ain't* going to go nowhere. I learned that from [Booker T.'s drummer] Al Jackson. Playing with him that many years, you just learn how to keep the groove."

First listen to "Soul Man," and then start refining the moves on your fretboard. Remember, the scrapes are as important as the notes.

Memorable fills are a Cropper trademark, and those in "Soul Man" have a cool genesis. Ask Steve if he used a slide to get his stinging tone and he'll tell you, "Well, I did and I didn't. I used a Zippo cigarette lighter! I kept it right on my knee—I just picked it up and played it. Couldn't move too much, 'cause it would vibrate off." Examples 2a and 2b illustrate two of Cropper's let's-toy-with-the-rhythm "Soul Man" fills. No Zippo on hand? Almost any blunt metal object will work; just keep your tone bright and whining.

Ex. 2a **Ex. 2b**

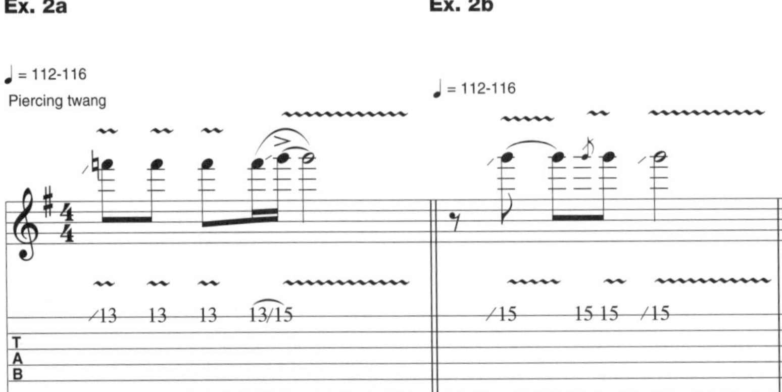

Sliding 6ths are another hallmark of the classic Cropper style. "Soul Man" opens with a figure like the one in Ex. 3. Keep your fingers glued to the 1st and 3rd strings. Despite its seesaw melody, the lick is played out of a single major-6th shape that you slide up and down the fretboard. Your right hand generates the melody—use a combination of flatpick and middle finger and let everything ring out. Note the implied chords in parentheses.

Hendrix borrowed ideas from Cropper. Listen to Jimi's intro in "Night Bird Flying" (from *The Cry of Love*) and compare it to the "Soul Man" intro. Déjà vu?

Ex. 3

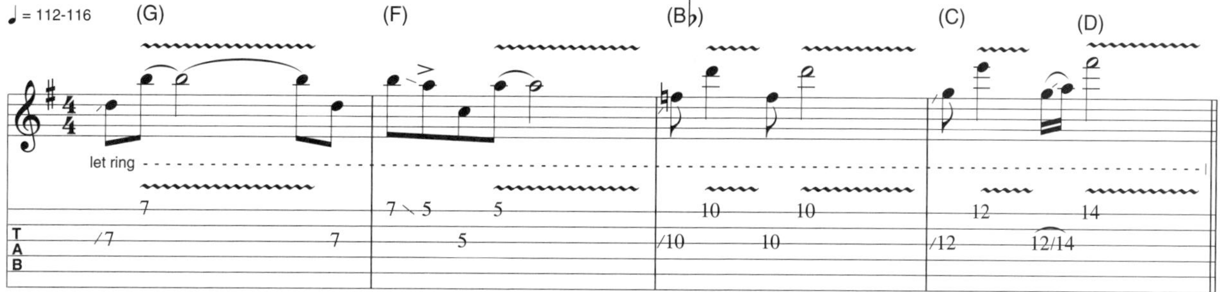

Cropper also featured 6ths in Otis Redding's "(Sittin' on) the Dock of the Bay." Example 4 occurs at the end of the bridge. When sliding these intervals, Steve sometimes picks only the top note while slurring the lower one, as in beat *three* of bars 1 and 2. Such subtleties give a part dynamics and dimension.

"I love playing ballads," Steve reveals. "It's my favorite thing. Within a rhythm pattern, I play things you could almost call horn lines. Many times the horns doubled what I did—we'd build the whole horn arrangement around my guitar."

Ex. 4

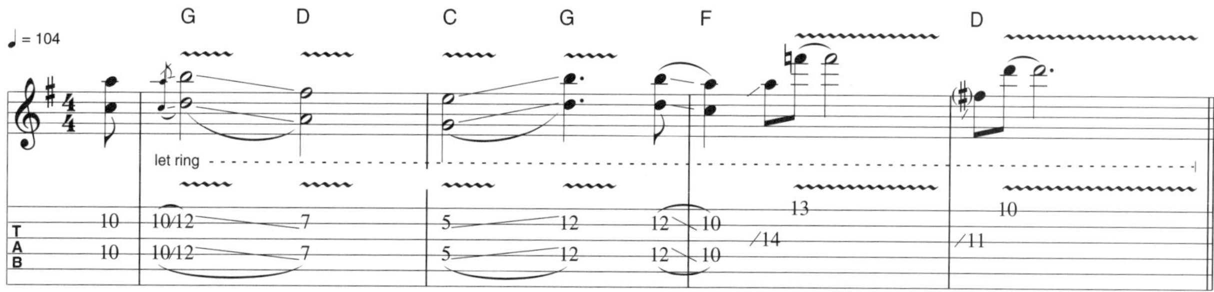

Often Cropper's Tele joins the singer in a duet. "It comes out that way because I'm always hearing a countermelody to what the vocalist is doing," Steve says. "I don't like doing sessions where the singer is not singing. Just sitting and playing means nothing. I'm happy when I work in and around the melody, doing little accents and filling the holes." The refrain fill in "Dock of the Bay" (Ex. 5) is a perfect example of Cropper's melodic duet style. Dig how he ends on *F#*—the major 9—against the *E* chord.

There's a fine line between orbiting the melody and getting in the way. Since R&B is about the singer and the song, it's essential to focus on the big picture. "I started doing that at a very early age," says Steve. "It stems from listening to what other people are doing instead of just what I'm playing. It takes a trained ear to hear everything at once—the singer, the bass, the drum beat, the piano parts—and then find a hole for yourself. If you're not conscious of what everybody's doing, you're going to step on someone. I think of it as *weaving* melodic fills. You develop an instinct for it. I'd realize that Booker or Isaac Hayes was going to play a piano fill and get off of my lick real quick."

Ex. 5

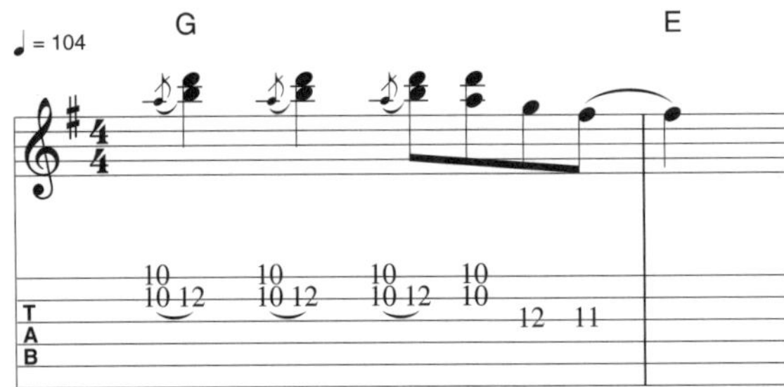

Cropper knows his share of sly chordal tricks. Example 6 is a neat descending passage from "Soul Dressing"—a slinky Booker T. & the MG's tune. The figure outlines a *Gm–Gm/maj7–Gm7–C9* progression. To get an authentically dry, scratchy tone, use your bridge pickup and a bright amp setting, and apply generous amounts of funky right-hand palm muting. Barre at the 3rd fret to facilitate the second pull-off.

Ex. 6

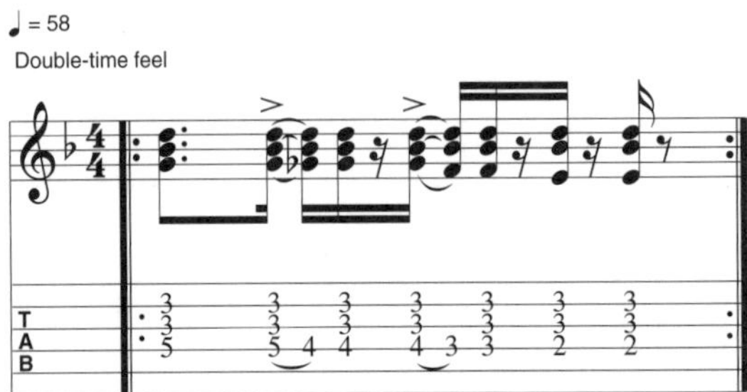

Here's another cool chord thang: Cropper's chromatic tremolo passage in Otis' impassioned "These Arms of Mine." Example 7a illustrates Cropper's simple but effective 12/8 arpeggios (bars 3 and 4)—a mainstay in many Otis ballads, including "Pain in My Heart," "Come to Me," "That's How Strong My Love Is," "That's What My Heart Needs," "Chained and Bound," and "I've Been Loving You Too Long (to Stop Now)." Dig how the four notes in bars 1 and 2 imply the entire progression in Ex. 7b. It's Cropper's economy of motion at work again.

Ex. 7a

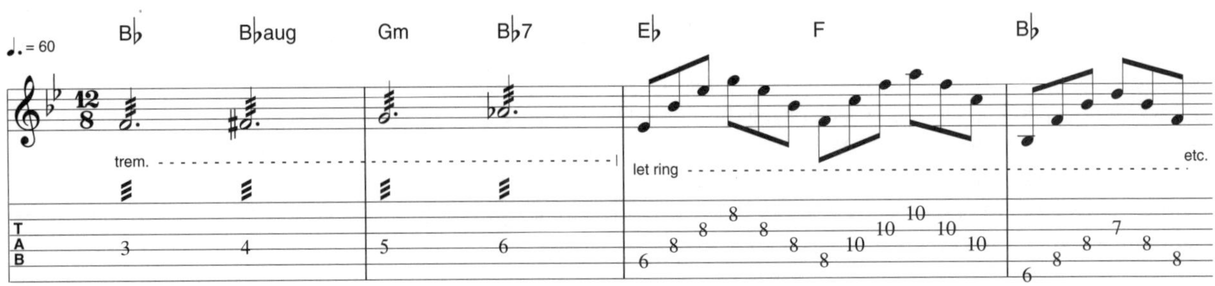

Ex. 7b

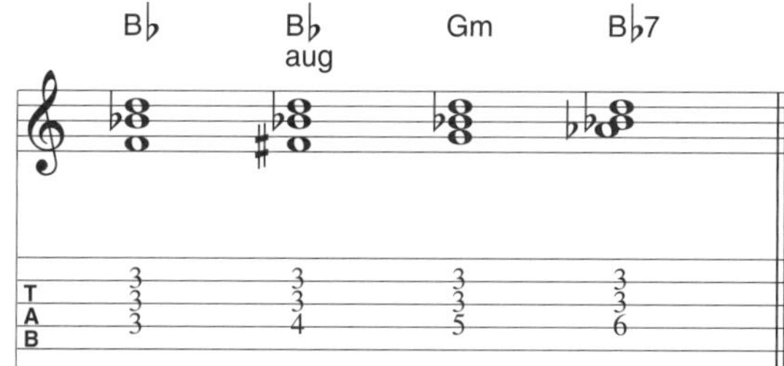

The MG's' "Behave Yourself" features a bluesy chord passage that ends in a horn-like *F6* gliss (Ex. 8). Yeah—another application for those 6ths. "A big part of the MG's sound comes from me doubling Duck Dunn's bass line *exactly*," says Cropper. This technique produces tight, punchy riffs an octave apart. In "Behave Yourself," Dunn and Cropper double the line in Ex. 9.

Ex. 8

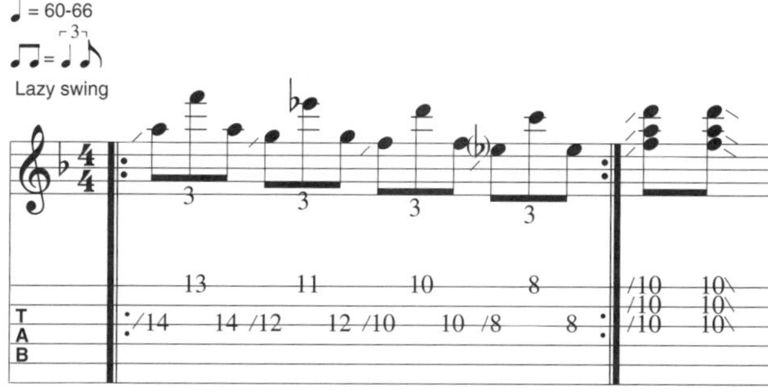

Ex. 9

The MG's' chugging "Time Is Tight" features lockstep bass and guitar in one of the coolest R&B riffs ever (Ex. 10). Try playing this syncopated groove with a friend (the bass takes the bottom line only). The sonic recipe: Damp down a bright tone with your right-hand palm so you get a dark yet crunchy sound.

Ex. 10

Otis Redding's "I Can't Turn You Loose" features a cooking riff, with Dunn and Cropper again doubling parts (Ex. 11). The classic soul turnaround (bar 1) is played in unison with bass and horns.

Ex. 11

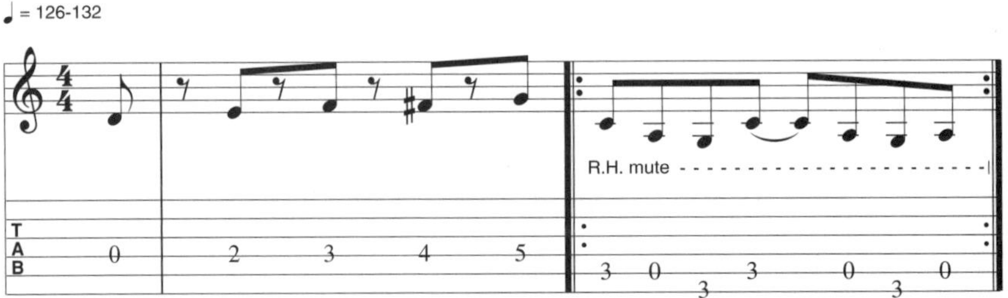

The MG's excelled at percolating, good-time instrumentals. One such tune—"Jellybread"—contains a bluesy chord vamp (Ex. 12) that balances fast hammers and pulls with wide-open space. Since the MG's showcased Booker T.'s organ and often featured horns, the compositions were typically in "flat" keys associated with those instruments (say, *F*, *B♭*, and *E♭*, rather than the guitar-friendly "sharp" keys of *E* and *A*). Cropper figured out how to incorporate open strings into his riffs anyway. Example 13, also from "Jellybread," lets you hammer from an open *E* into the riff's *F* downbeat for a cool walking bass sound. The riff works in *B♭* too: Just move it one string-set higher—so you're hammering off the 5th string—and away you go.

Ex. 12

Ex. 13

In "Mo-Onions," a follow-up to "Green Onions," Cropper again slips open strings into a keyboard riff, as in Ex. 14. This versatile minor-key line works in many settings. The half-fretted notes on the "and" of *one* (bars 1 and 2) are the kind of little subtleties that spell the difference between good and great. Try this with and without a right-hand mute.

Ex. 14

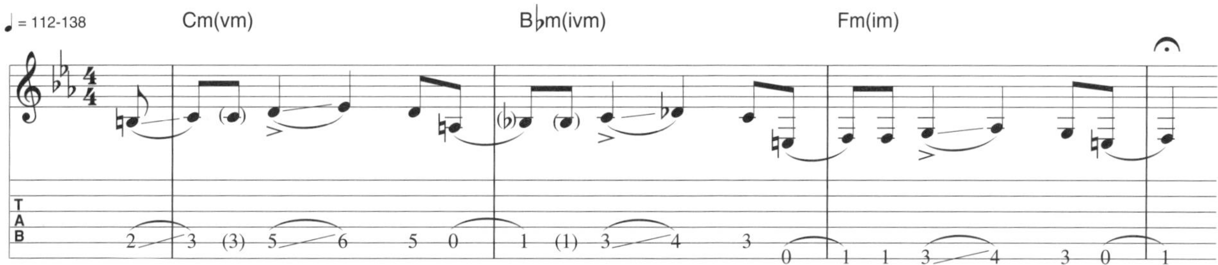

Cropper is not one for taking extended leads. "I've never looked at myself as a soloist. I really shy away from that. I'll take a solo—four or eight bars—and do what I do. But be a lead picker? These guys in Nashville literally amaze me, some of the stuff they pull off. I admire their technical ability—it's fantastic. But I take a lot of pride in what I do—I can keep time with the best of them. I've played with a lot of musicians who cannot keep time on their own."

When Cropper does take a lead, he's often fond of repeating a phrase against different chords. The bare-wire double-stops in Ex. 15 recall "Mo-Onions." To experience the tangy dissonance of the quarter-bends, let them hang starkly against the chords.

Ex. 15

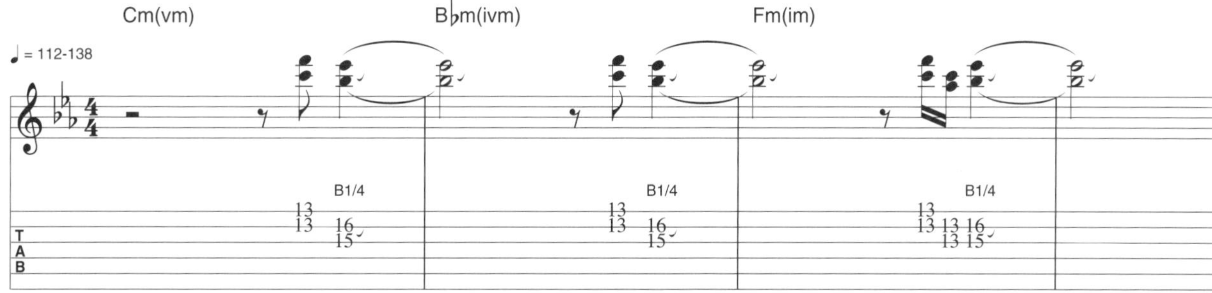

If there's a classic Cropper lead lick, Ex. 16 is it. Featured in "Green Onions," this snarling Tele stab is pure Memphis.

Ex. 16

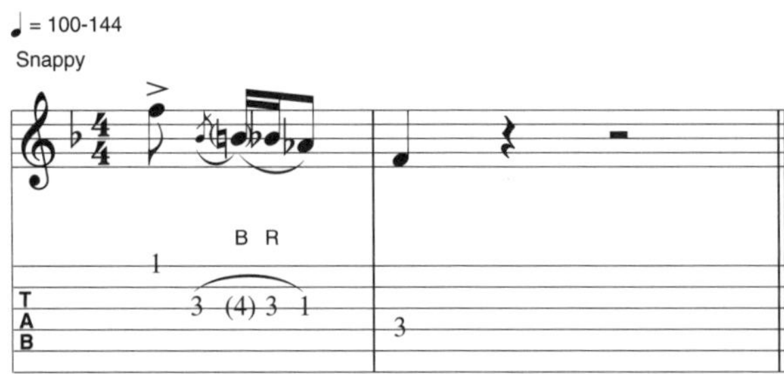

Sometimes Steve liked to tune to an open *E* chord, a technique he used in "I've Been Loving You Too Long (to Stop Now)." It sure simplifies those arpeggiated barre chords. The approach has gospel roots, says Cropper. "We used to do a thing where we'd put some vibrato on and tune down to *D*—made this wonderful sound for church stuff." Example 17—a chord excerpt from "Loving You Too Long"—is quintessential Stax harmony. Its simplicity belies its evocative power. Give the chords a whirl—slowly now—and see if you don't picture a dimly lit club wrapped in a blue haze of cigarette smoke. See the red leatherette booths? The old Wurlitzer jukebox? The sultry women clustered at the bar gazing with half-lidded eyes at the bandstand?

Ex. 17

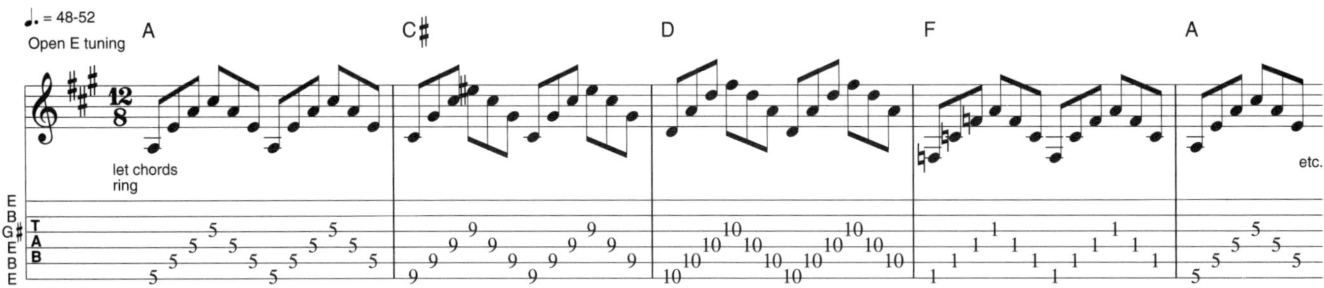

Cropper also used an open-*E* tuning in "Ole Man Trouble." The main riff (Ex. 18) has an almost bottleneck sound. "I stretched out," chuckles Cropper. "People would go, 'What's *that*?' The difference was I tuned to a chord, heh, heh."

Cropper slings a Tele-style Peavey these days. In the Stax years, however, it was a Fender Esquire or white Tele through a little Fender Harvard amp. Later, seeking more power, Steve settled on a Fender Super Reverb. Palm muting wasn't his only funk tool: "I used to leave my strings on until they broke—sometimes a couple of months. Seems like the more grit and grime that got on there, the better they sounded. I love that muted tone."

Ex. 18

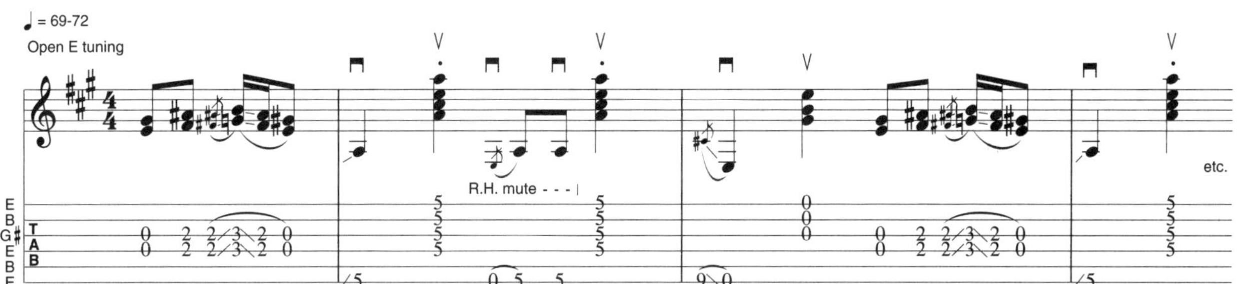

KEITH RICHARDS

Rhythm of a Rolling Stone

BY JOE DELORO

Keith Richards

Blazing a gold and platinum trail through the pop jungles of the world since the 1960s, the Rolling Stones long ago carved their claim to the title "World's Greatest Rock 'n' Roll Band." And, through dozens of albums and a seemingly endless list of hit singles, one thing has remained constant: their multi-styled, guitar-driven sound. In this lesson we're focusing on the style of the Stones' chief engineer and designated driver, Keith Richards.

In a December 1978 *Guitar Player* interview bassist Bill Wyman described Keith's role like this: "Our band does not follow the drummer; our drummer follows the rhythm guitarist."

The best way to understand Keith's contribution is to listen to the music. Notice how the riffs, chords, and solos draw on a wide variety of influences (blues, R&B, rock 'n' roll, country-western, reggae) and are blended with great feel, interplay, and texture.

In a November 1977 *Guitar Player* story, Keith said: "What's interesting about rock 'n' roll for me, and particularly for guitarists, is that if there are two guitarists and they're playing well together and really jell, there seem to be infinite possibilities open. It comes to the point where you're not conscious anymore of who's doing what. It's not at all a split thing. It's like two instruments becoming one sound."

More often than not, the Stones' sound stays on course by avoiding the standard back-to-front rhythm and lead guitar approach typical of so much pop music. With that in mind, let's look at some of the techniques Keith uses to create such memorable electric guitar parts.

Example 1 starts us up with a riff reminiscent of the intro to the Stones' second U.S. single, "It's All Over Now." The song was recorded in Chicago at Chess Records (the studio home of their heroes, Muddy Waters and Howlin' Wolf) at the end of their first U.S. tour in 1964.

Notice that the first two chords are inverted (no root in the bass), while the second two are in root position. This creates a streamlined sound. By using these fingerings and keeping the same number of strings for each pair of chords, you get nice melodic voice-leading between chords. Also important here is the broken chord strumming in the theme and variation phrasing.

Of course, without an electric 12-string lead—played by Brian Jones in the recording—the overall effect would be lost. By starting Ex. 1's figures on beat *two*, the lead guitar and rhythm guitar take turns in the sonic spotlight. It's a great example of effective simplicity. The final *D* chord creates a nice tonal ambiguity by suggesting a key change from *C* to *G*.

Ex. 1

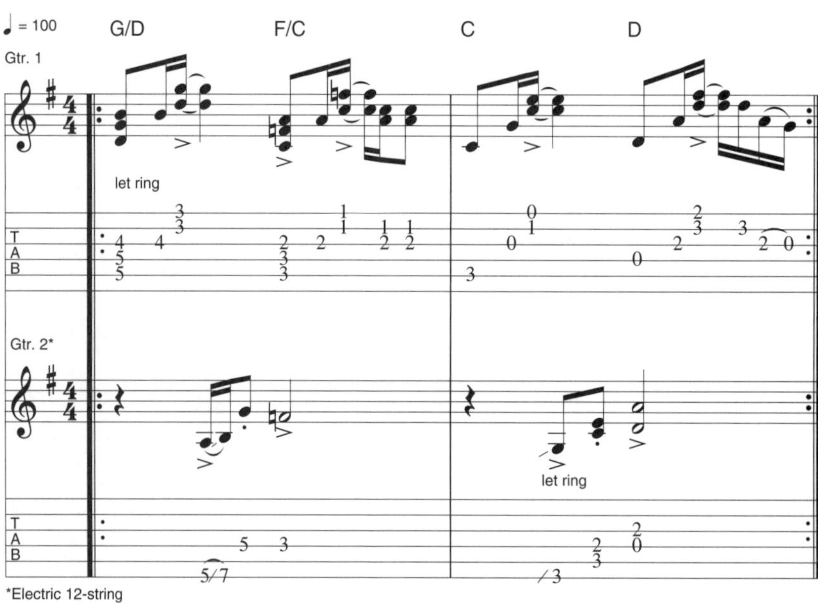

"Get Off of My Cloud," the follow-up to "Satisfaction," was the second consecutive No. 1 U.S. single for the band. Example 2 is based on the main rhythm groove—again, the rhythm part is on guitar 1, the 12-string part on guitar 2. With a faster tempo than Ex. 1 and a more melodic line from guitar 2, this part shows some of the versatility of this arranging style. Notice how the rhythm guitar heavies up the backbeat, R&B–style, by emphasizing beats *two* and *four* with damped chords.

Ex. 2

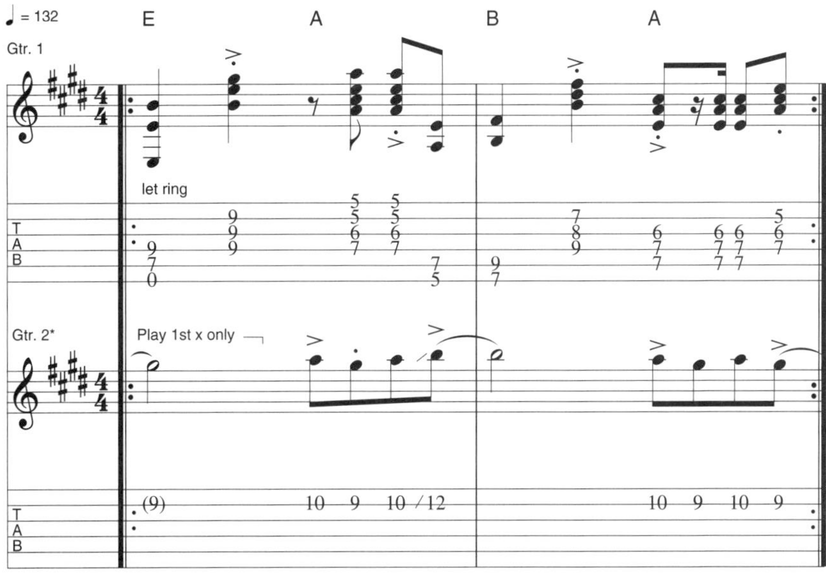

The idea behind Ex. 3 is "It's Not Easy," a track from the Stones' seventh album, *Aftermath*. By combining ultra-laid-back, almost shuffling blues lines on guitar 1 with a Chuck Berry rhythm in straight eighths on guitar 2, a great groove is born. Be patient with the rhythm guitar part if you're new to the style. Work towards clarity and balance between palm muting and left-hand damping.

Ex. 3

In July '69 "Honky Tonk Women" checked in at No. 1 and stayed there for a month. It featured a new addition to the Stones' guitar sound, open-*G* tuning. It was also the first single to include Mick Taylor, Brian Jones's replacement. Taylor contributed some of the lead parts after Richards and the band had laid down the initial backing tracks.

Ex. 4a will give you an idea of how Keith created his intro part. Try it with hybrid picking, using your pick and your middle fingers to pluck the string pairs.

Ex. 4a

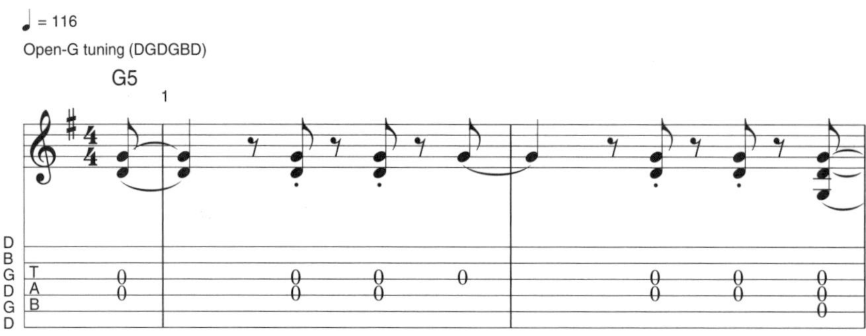

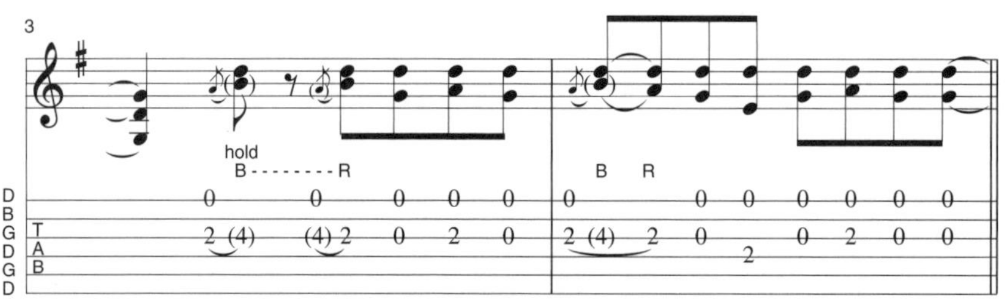

Keith's approach to the first verse is profiled in Ex. 4b. Like his earlier work with Jones, he phrases against Jagger's vocals with powerful simplicity. In this song he let drummer Charlie Watts and Wyman carry the rhythm while he focused on creating tension and release with brief pickups to chord changes that lead in and out of suspensions.

Example 5 offers a creative approach to the shuffle rhythm. With a capo at the 7th fret and an *A–Asus2* chord change at beat *three*, this routine rhythm is given a fresh twist along the lines of one of the best-known titles from *Let It Bleed*, "Midnight Rambler." Be sure to damp the *A* chord on beat *three* before going to *Asus2*.

Illustrating Keith's melodic rhythm style, Examples 6a and 6b are based on the two intro progressions of "Brown Sugar," the 1969 No. 1 single from *Sticky Fingers*. Another great example of Keith's artistry with open-*G* tuning, the rhythm part stays melodic at all times by using chord positions that access different notes along the 2nd string. Example 6b also shows how Keith keeps things harmonically fresh during the second progression by shifting the tonal center up a minor 3rd to *E♭*.

Ex. 4b

Ex. 5

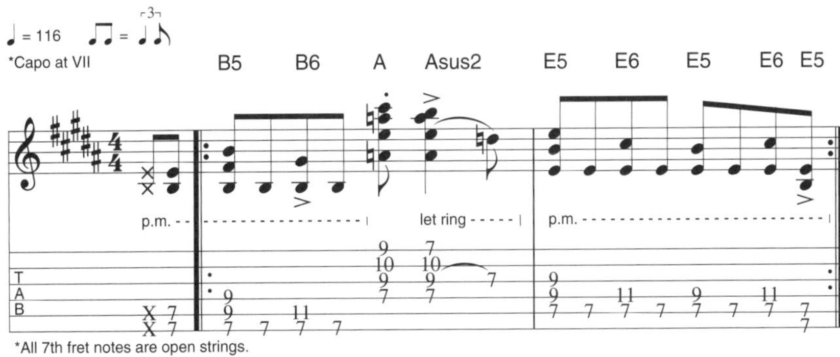

*All 7th fret notes are open strings.

Ex. 6a

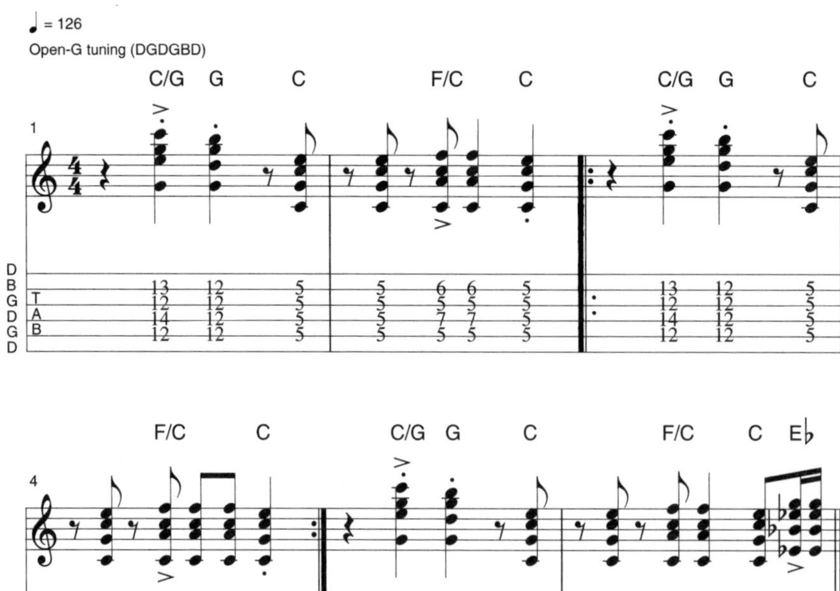
♩ = 126
Open-G tuning (DGDGBD)
C/G G C F/C C C/G G C
F/C C C/G G C F/C C E♭

Ex. 6b

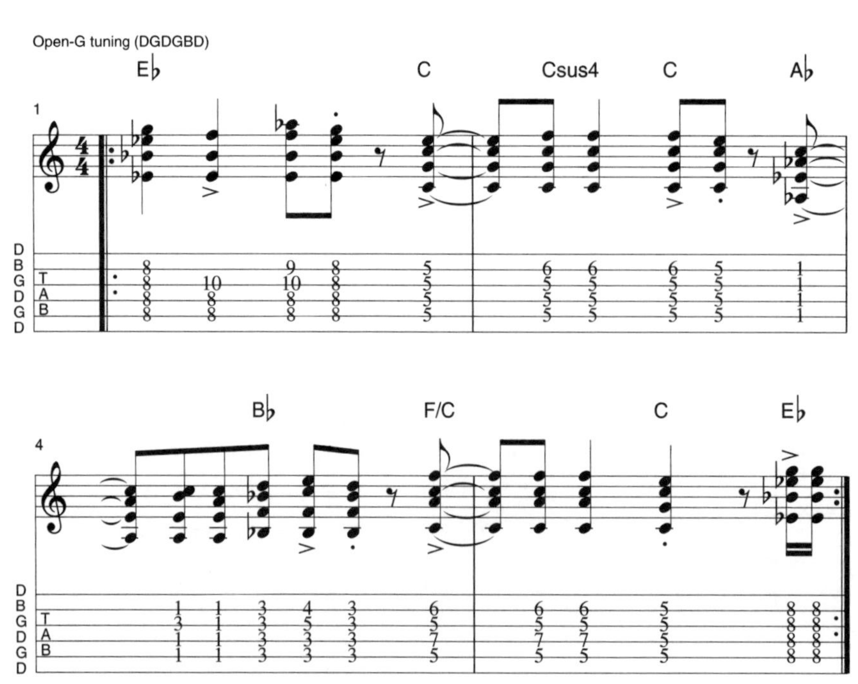
Open-G tuning (DGDGBD)
E♭ C Csus4 C A♭
B♭ F/C C E♭

The intro to "Can't You Hear Me Knockin'" is the basis of Ex. 7a. You start off playing rhythm, move to a lead motif in bar 2, go back to rhythm for two bars, then finish with three lead motifs in a row. The lead figures are similar melodically, but each starts in a different part of the measure. All these elements, plus the 16th-note syncopations that run throughout the part, build tension and propel the music.

Ex. 7a

Example 7b looks in on the verse. Here the guitar 1 part alternates between a melody line and some more signature lead/rhythm fills. Guitar 2 is similar to Mick Taylor's rhythm part. Notice how both parts complement each other by using similar accents, scratching, and rests.

Ex. 7b

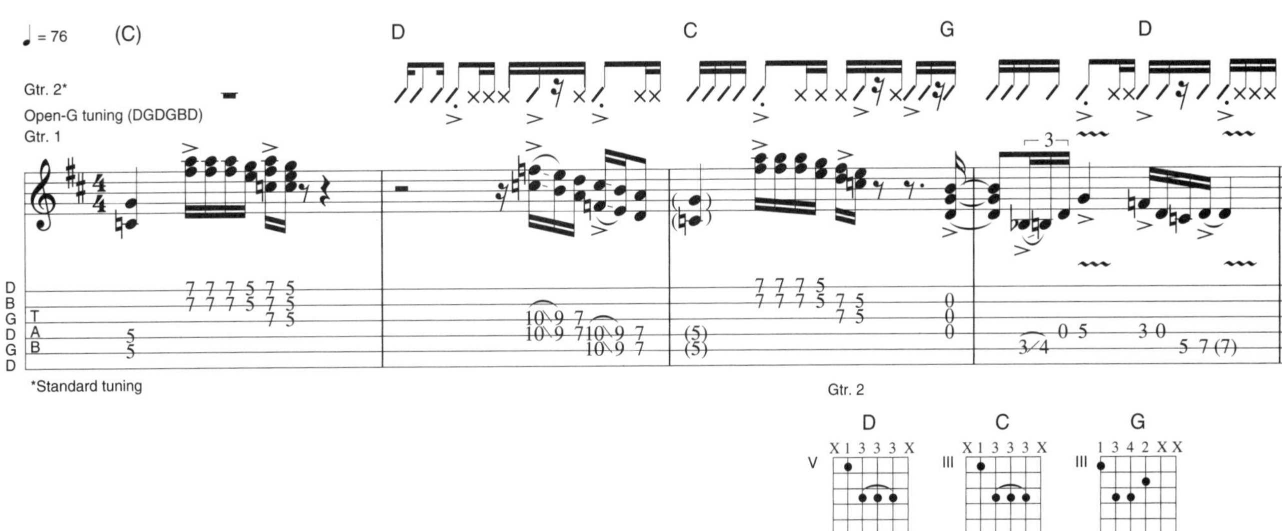

Ex. 8a will remind you of the intro to "Tumblin' Dice" from the Stones' 1972 album *Exile on Main Street*. In open-*G* tuning and capoed at the 4th fret, the part begins with a classic harmonized R&B-style lick before settling into a soulful rhythm groove. Be sure to observe the damping instructions to keep the part crisp.

Ex. 8a

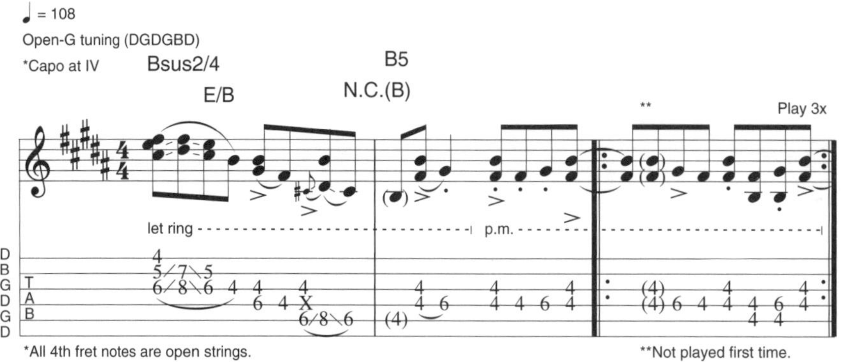

Examples 8b and 8c are based on verses 1 and 3. The main difference between the two examples is in their final measures. Example 8b features the main progression, while Ex. 8c introduces a music hook that works in harmony with the vocals.

Ex. 8b

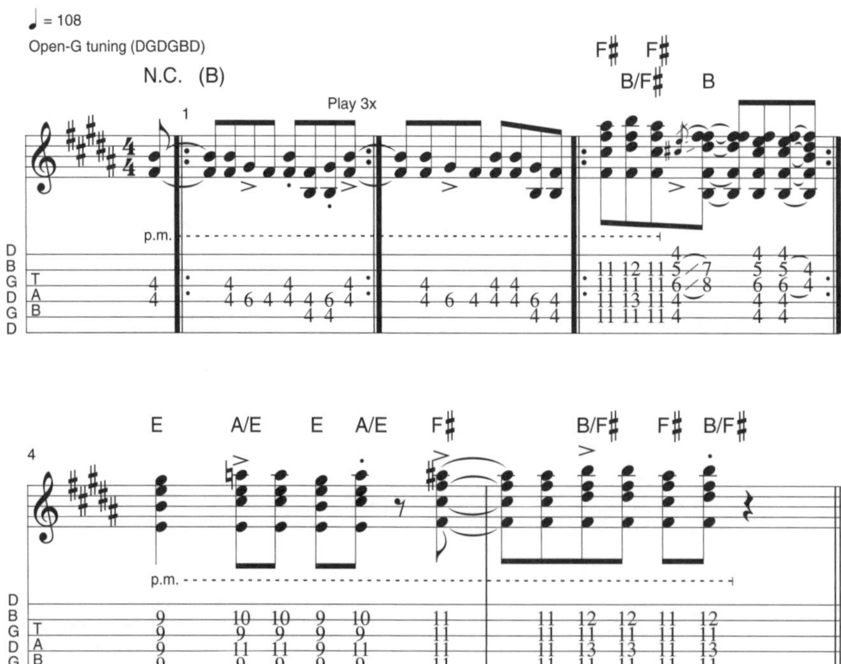

Ex. 8c

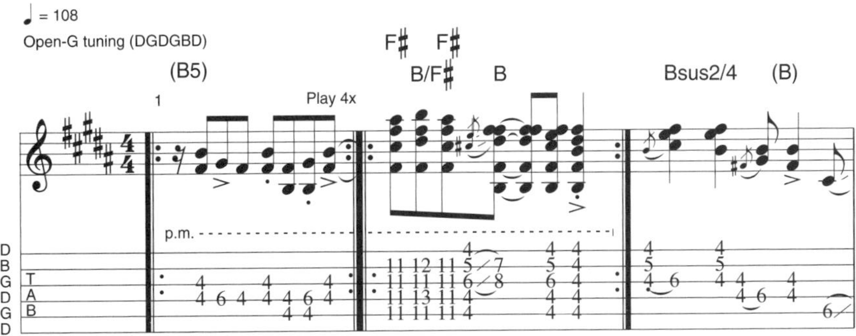

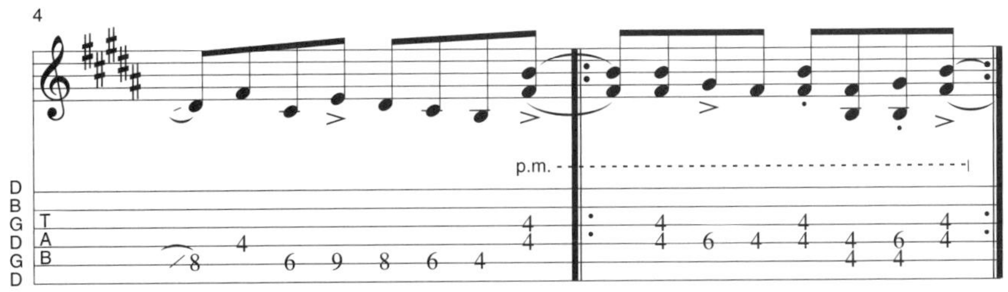

Example 9 highlights Keith's approach to the intro rhythm of "Beast of Burden," from 1978's *Some Girls*. It's pretty straightforward except for the first figure, a hammer-on from *B* to *E/B*. It may take a little practice to get the second chord to ring fully. This is one more illustration of the way Keith's syncopated style drives a rhythm part with great feel.

Ex. 9

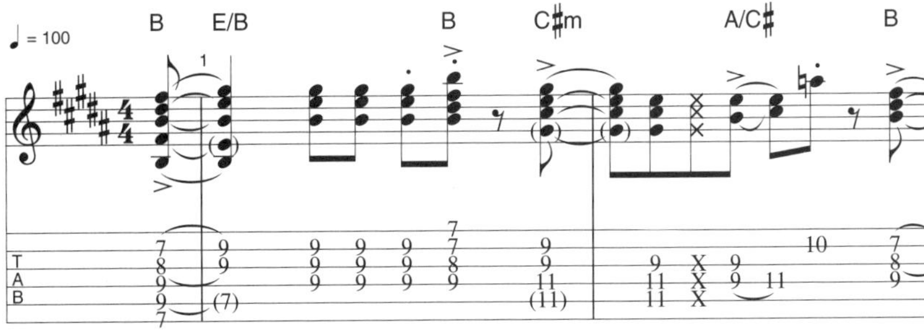

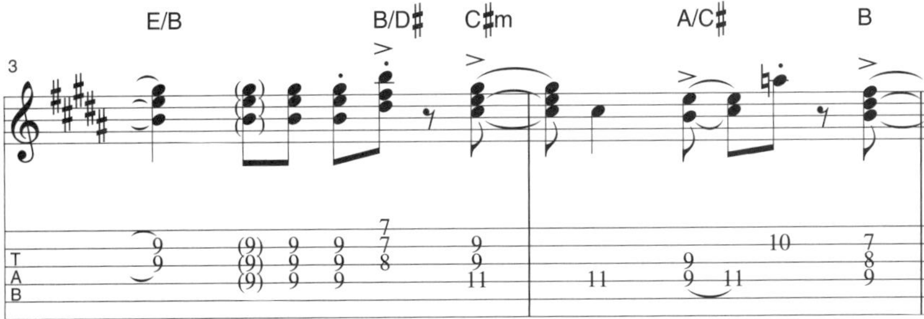

THE RICHARDS SOUND

Freshness guaranteed: "I treat each track, each song, completely different. If I'm using a certain sound, a certain amp and guitar, on one track, I'll deliberately break that all down and set something else for the next track. Just so it's not all sounding alike, and because that's the only way you can learn new things—by constantly trying out new things." (*Guitar Player*, November '77)

Small is beautiful: "You can get very powerful-sounding recordings playing very quietly, and with relatively small amps. Small amps turned way up have the tension you're trying to get anyway, and it sounds big." (*Guitar Player*, April '83)

Distortion distinction: "Traditionally, I'd set up that Fender Twin and maybe slave a little Champ. I've always found that a really good distortion needs to come from two different places. Of course, that's not true for "Satisfaction," where it's an obvious thing, but you want some distortion and some clarity at the same time where you need it, so I'd rather put it through two amps and overload one of them." (*Guitar Player*, December '92)

Example 10 covers the first four bars of the intro to "Start Me Up," from 1981's *Tattoo You*. Again in open-*G* tuning, the first two measures harmonize the song's title melody; the second two switch over to a Chuck Berry rhythm with lots of sauce. This progression also acts as the foundation for the verses.

Ex. 10

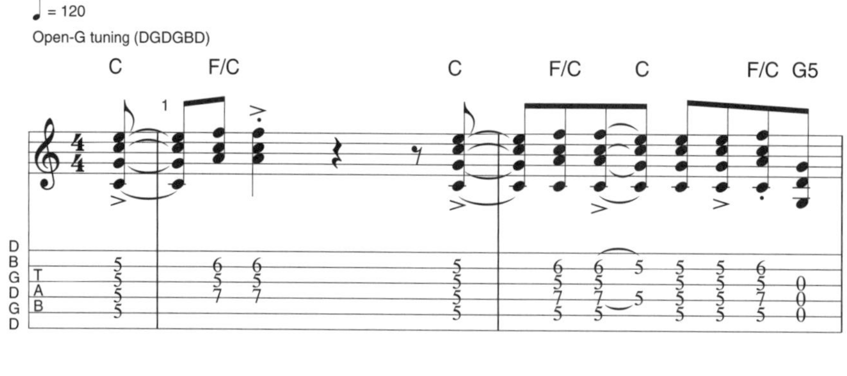

Set on an R&B/calypso groove alongside jazz great Sonny Rollins' tenor sax solos, "Waiting on a Friend" rides in style as the final track on *Tattoo You*. Keith's harmonic ideas for the intro/chorus rhythm are featured in Ex. 11. Notice how the added 9th and 6th extensions give this part just the right amount of tension.

Ex. 11

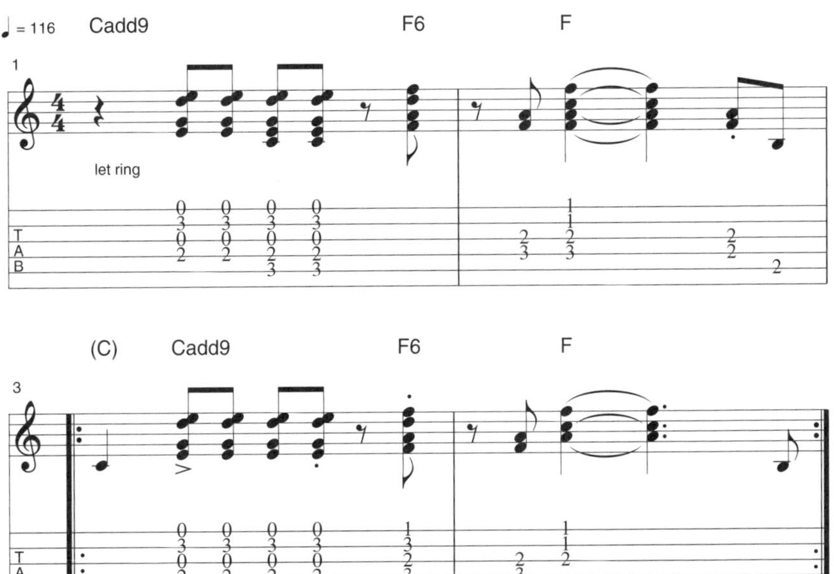

Ex. 12 bids farewell with moves featured in "You Got Me Rocking," from 1994's *Voodoo Lounge*. Alternating between *D5* and *Dsus4* in open-*G* tuning, it makes its case with pull-offs.

Ex. 12

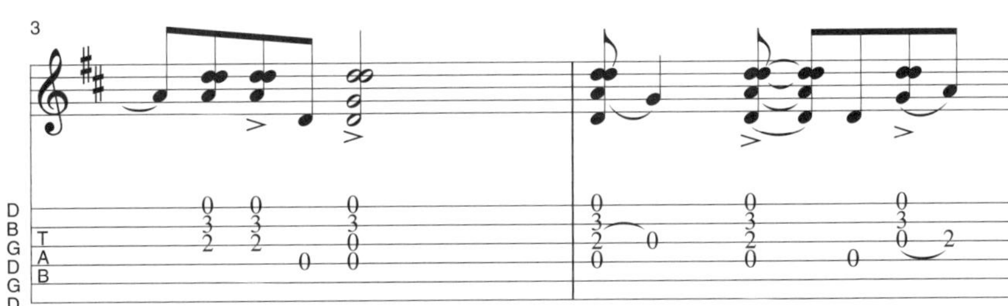

DAY ON THE GREEN

A Green Day Lesson

BY JESSE GRESS

Billie Joe Armstrong

Nobody plays rhythm like Pete Townshend, except maybe . . . Green Day's Billie Joe Armstrong?! Before condemning this declaration as way too rash, commit an hour or so to digesting the following Green Day rhythm guitar primer.

Within this crash course you'll discover evidence of vintage Who and Kinks power pop, Pistols-style bollocks-to-the-wall chordal assaults, and even an occasional nod to Van Halen, all reminiscent of the band's early '90s sound as chronicled on the *1,039/Smoothed Out Slappy Hours* compilation. Sometime between then and 1994's *Dookie*, Green Day engineered a stylistic overhaul that stripped down many of these elements and all but eliminated guitar solos. Their adolescent themes and Beatley harmonies were recast over speedy, fat-sounding chordal riffs.

One factor has remained constant. Billie Joe's relentless rhythm guitar drives the band. Devoid of vocal melodies, the following stylistic examples may seem generic or derivative, but therein lies the challenge to bring them to life. Think of each as a road map to an exuberant performance. The benefits range from learning the basics or a few new tricks to rediscovering the inherent giddiness in banging out simple chord forms.

Chord Library

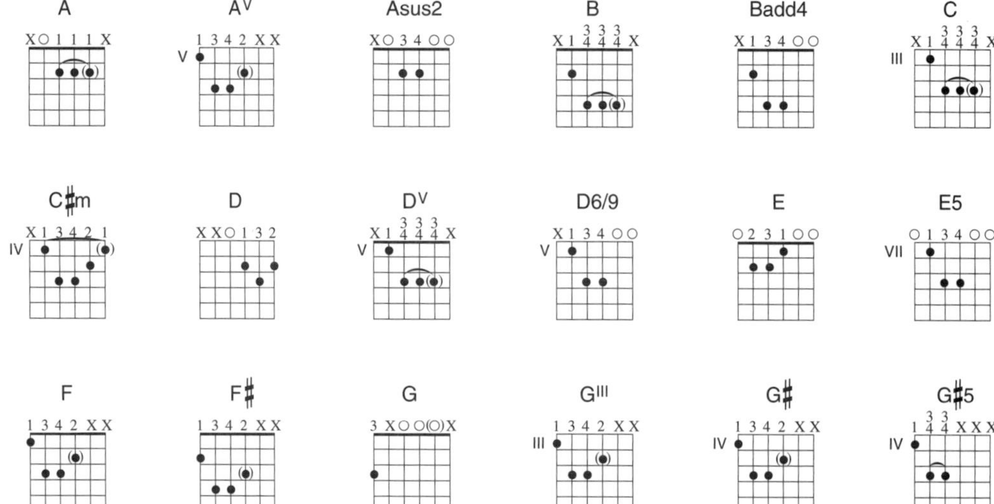

Examples 1–6 are notated using slash rhythms. The chord forms are listed alphabetically in the preceding chord library. Examples 1a–1g exploit the same rhythm motif, a Green Day staple found in such songs as "Judge's Daughter," "Why Do You Want Him?" "Only of You," "Dry Ice," and "I Want To Be Alone." Root motion outlines the progressions V–IV–I–V, I–VI–IV–V, I–V–III–IV, I–II–IV–V, I–III–IV–I, I–III–IV–V, and IV–V–I–VI respectively.

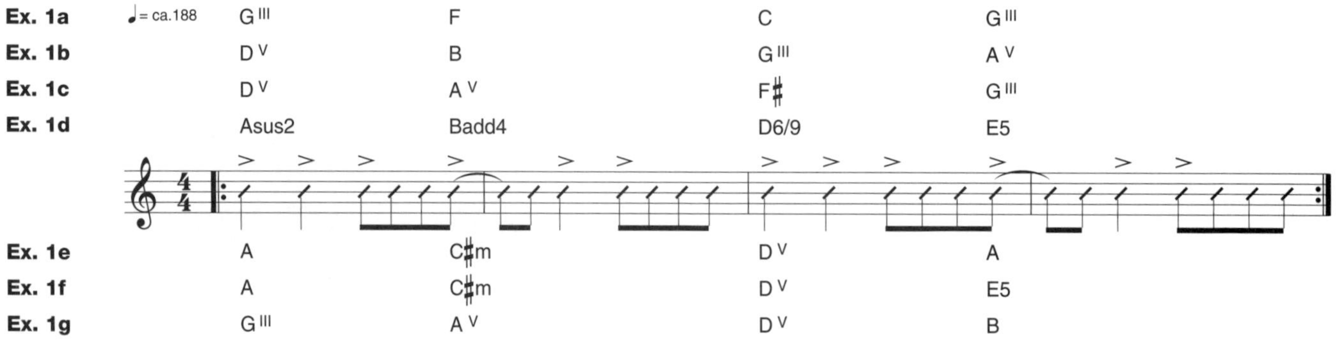

Example 2a features the same rhythm with twice the duration (two bars) for each chord. The slight rhythmic alteration in Ex. 2b outlines a III–I–V progression with a neutered (no 3rd) III chord (*G#5*).

Ex. 2a

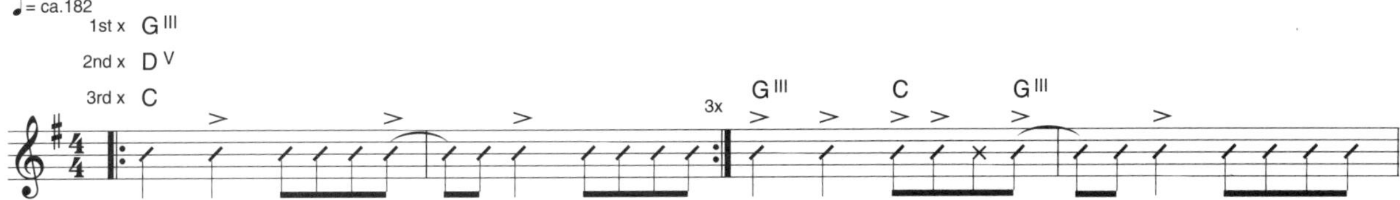

Ex. 2b

Typical of a Billie Joe "chord solo," Ex. 3a offers a look at open passing chords, those naturally occurring open strings that sound en route to the next chord. Apply the concept to other examples as you see fit. The "X" note heads in the Townshendesque power-chord riffs of Ex. 3b and 3c indicate muted, not open, strings as in the previous example. Both use I–♭VII–IV progressions, another Green Day hallmark.

Ex. 3a

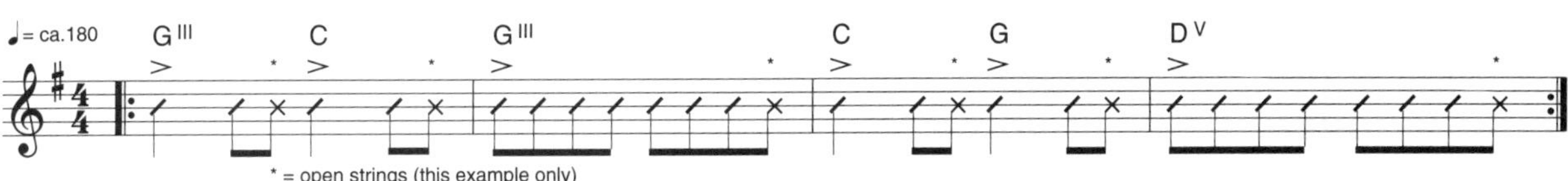

Ex. 3b

Ex. 3c

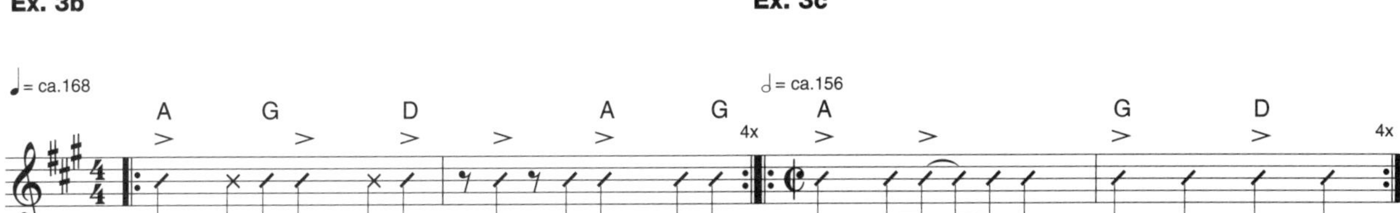

Subtle rhythmic variations shape the I–♭VII–IV riff in Ex. 4a, while Ex. 4b transposes the progression to *B* with a rare swing-eighth injection.

Ex. 4a

Ex. 4b

♩= ca.178 E E⑥ open D A E⑥ open 4x

♩= ca.148 B A E 4x

The Who-ish Ex. 5a is a cranked-up I–V–IV figure, while Ex. 5b serves up a syncopated I–IV–♭VII–I.

Ex. 5a

Ex. 5b

The four-bar phrase in Ex. 6a chugs solidly on the I except for the brief ♭VII–IV punctuation in bar 3. Play the "X" note heads in Ex. 6b as either muted or open strings. Note the major III chord (*G♯*) in the I–III–IV progression. Example 6c introduces a rarity in Green Day music: rests. The open spaces between syncopated chords build plenty of rhythmic tension before resolving to straightahead eighth-notes in bar 4.

Lest you think that all Billie Joe does is pound out chords, consider Ex. 7, reminiscent of circa-1990 Green Day. Arpeggiating the root/5 chords against a droning open *G* string creates expanded harmonies. Top this off with the following flurry of 5th- and 7th-fret harmonies and you'll swear you can smell Van Halen nearby.

Ex. 7

Arpeggiated chordal figures were much more prominent in Green Day's earlier sound. Example 8 presents two more BJ-approved open string voicings: *Asus2* and the eerie *F♯add4*. Adding the open *E* creates *F♯7add4*. Try it.

Ex. 8

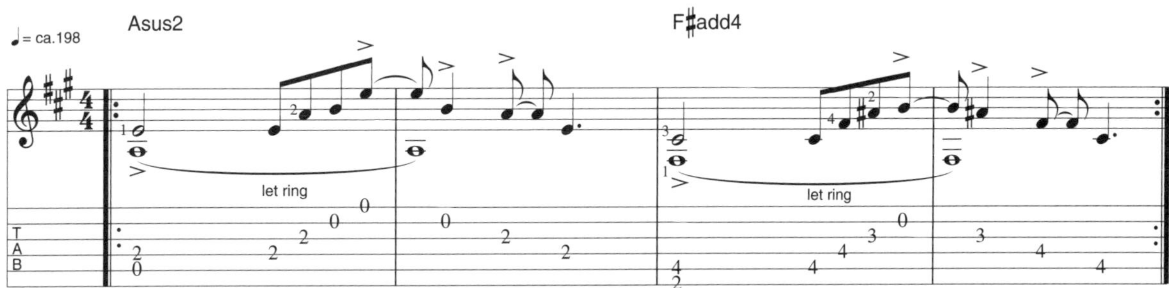

Examine the two single-note riffs derived from I–♭VII progressions in Examples 9a and 9b. Example 9a adds a 4 to the I chord and a ♯4 to the ♭VII chord. The 12/8 feel and ominous tonality in Ex. 9b impart a grungy mood.

Ex. 9a **Ex. 9b**

♩= ca.198 Dadd4 Csus♯4 ♩.= ca.62 G5 Fadd9 G5

let ring let ring

The introductory figure in Ex. 10a features a pedal *B5* chord against a moving bass line, another favorite Townshend technique. Example 10b is a Sex Pistols–style approach to the old V–I.

Ex. 10a

Ex. 10b

Broken down to diads (double-stops, or two-note chords), Ex. 11 describes the harmonic climate over an extended (two bars each) I–♭VII progression. Fingerstyle double-stops in Ex. 12 create another Van Halen vibe, again over a I–♭VII movement.

Ex. 11

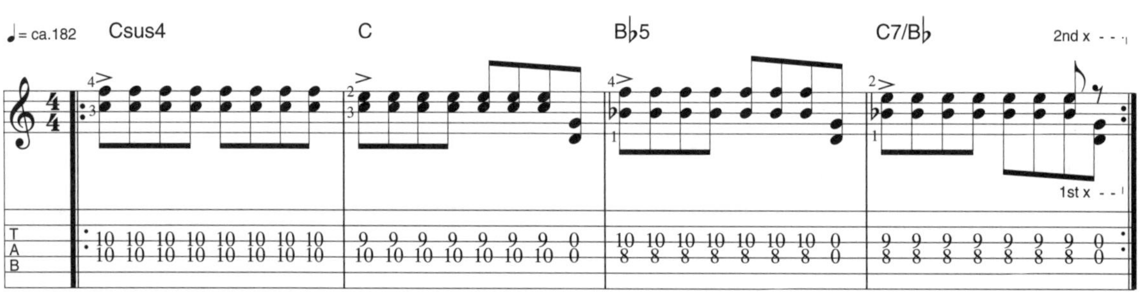

Ex. 12

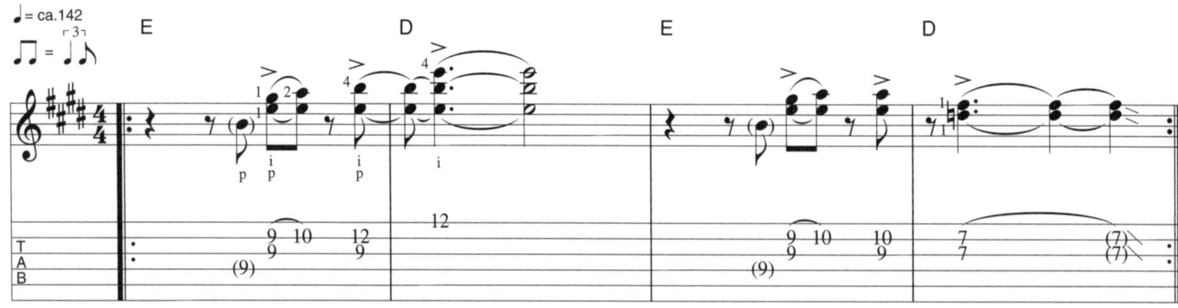

Example 13a transforms a *B* pentatonic minor line into a wicked chord riff in which each chord in bar 1 switches string groups. Examples 13b and 13c are killer one-bar hooks outlining I–V–♯IV–V and I–♭VII–I respectively.

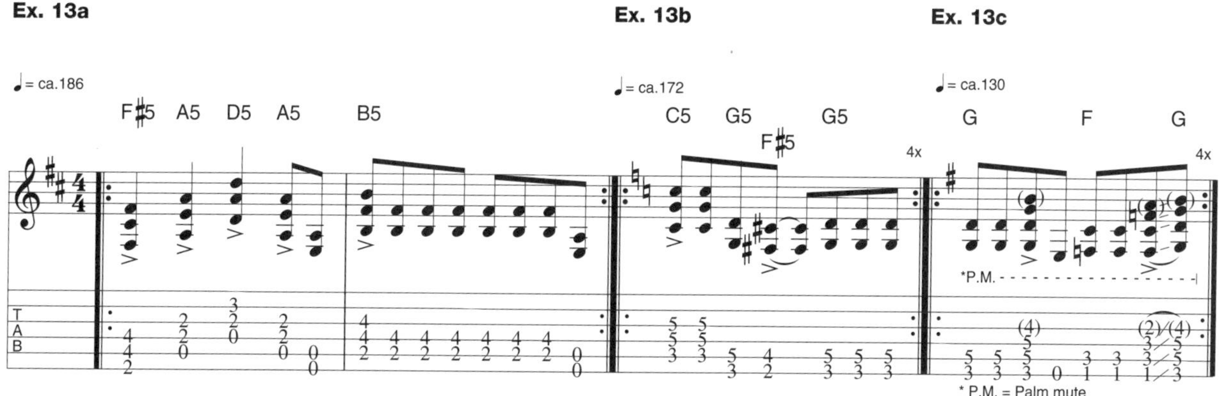

Single notes, double-stops, and chords are combined to various degrees in Examples 14a and 14b. The intense Yardbirds-style rave-up in Ex. 15a is recast as a single-note riff in Ex. 15b.

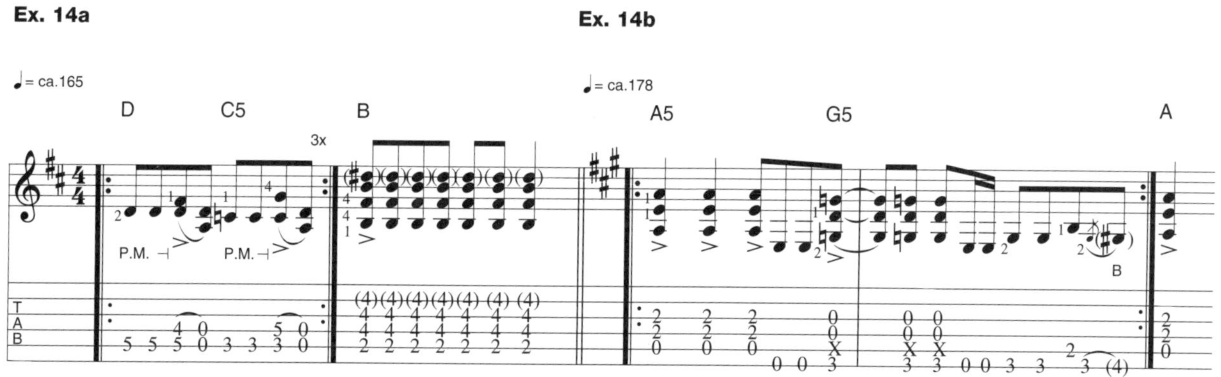

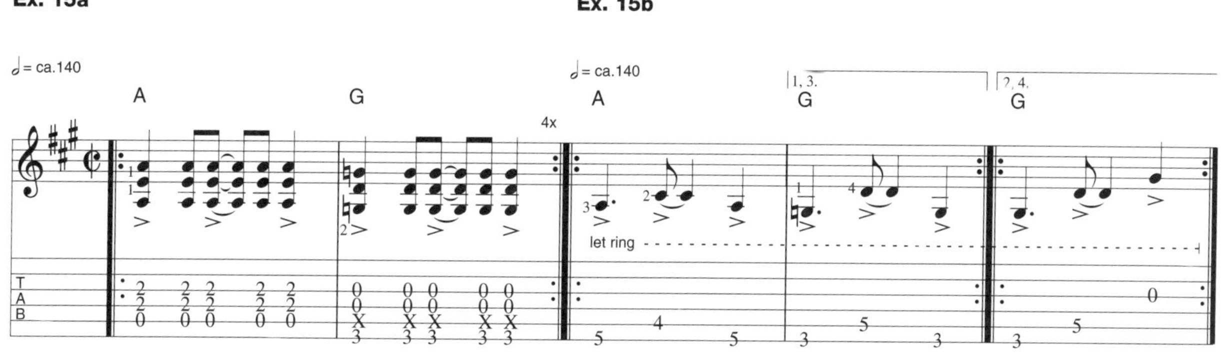

An uncharacteristically metal-like intro, Ex. 16 alternates single-note phrases with quick double-stops that pit the I and ♭VII chords against an open-*G* drone.

Ex. 16

Broken-chord figures that contrast muted bass lines with sharp chordal punctuations are among the most recognizable elements of BJ's current style. Example 17 illustrates with a I–V–VI–III–IV–I–V progression, while Ex. 18 puts I–V–VI–IV through similar paces.

So there you have it—a cavalcade of chordal cacophony that'd make Old Rubberwrist proud. Approach each example with unbridled passion, and you too could be Green for a Day!

Ex. 17

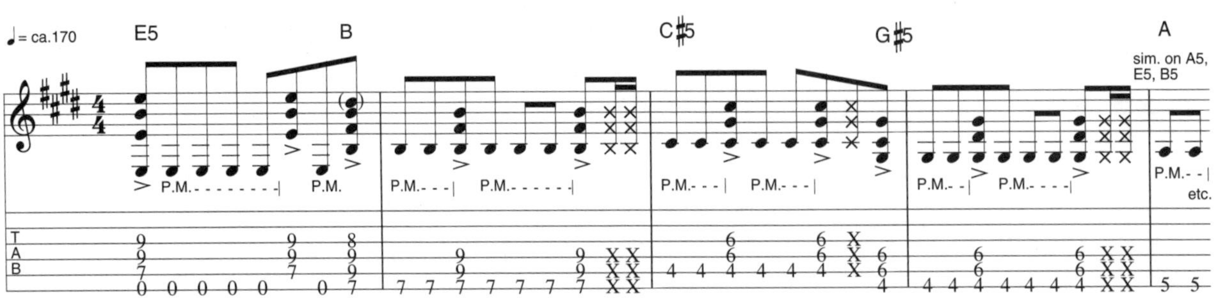

Ex. 18

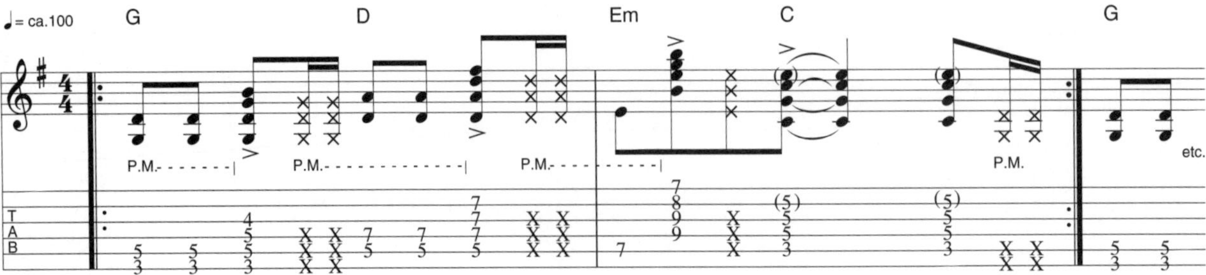

MASTER STROKES

A Rhythm Guitar Discography: Where to Hear Artists and Songs Mentioned in *How to Play Rhythm Guitar*

BLUES

Robert Johnson
King of the Delta Blues Singers Vol. 2, Columbia Legacy

T-Bone Walker
Midnight Blues, Complete Blues

Jimmy Rogers
w/Muddy Waters
The Best of Muddy Waters, Chess

Robert Jr. Lockwood
Steady Rollin' Man, Delmark

Freddie King
Let's Hide Away and Dance Away with Freddy King, King

FUNK

Nile Rodgers
w/Chic
The Very Best of Chic, Rhino

Al McKay
w/Earth, Wind & Fire
Spirit, Columbia/Legacy

Tony Maiden
w/Rufus
(both on MCA)
Rufus Featuring Chaka Khan
Rufusized

Al Ciner
w/Rufus
Rags to Rufus, MCA

Prince
1999, Warner Bros.

Roger Troutman
w/Zapp
Zapp, Warner Bros.

ROCK

P.I.L. (Public Image Ltd)
The Greatest Hits So Far, Virgin

XTC
Drums & Wires, Virgin

Defunkt
Avoid the Funk, Hannibal

Talking Heads
Remain in Light, Warner Bros.

Fishbone
Truth and Soul, Columbia

Red Hot Chili Peppers
The Red Hot Chili Peppers, EMI

Jane's Addiction
Ritual de lo Habitual, Warner Bros.

Sonic Youth
Daydream Nation, Geffen

My Bloody Valentine
Loveless, Sire

The Smiths
The Best of the Smiths (Volumes 1 and 2), Sire

Soundgarden
Ultramega OK, SST

Dinosaur Jr.
Where You Been?, Sire

Nirvana
In Utero, Geffen

Helmet
Helmet, Interscope

REGGAE

Burning Spear
Marcus Garvey, Mango

Toots & the Maytals
Time Tough: The Anthology, Island

Bob Marley & the Wailers
Rastaman Vibration, Island

RHYTHM KINGS

Steve Cropper
w/Booker T. & the MG's
Groovin', Rhino
w/Otis Redding
The Ultimate Otis Redding, Warner Bros.

Keith Richards
w/The Rolling Stones
(on ABKCO)
Hot Rocks, 1964–1971
More Hot Rocks (Big Hits and Fazed Cookies)
Aftermath
(on Virgin)
Exile on Main Street
Some Girls
Tattoo You
Voodoo Lounge

Green Day
1,039/Smoothed Out Slappy Hours, Lookout Records

PHOTO CREDITS

© FDR / Michael Ochs Archives.com, page 41
© Michael Ochs Archives.com, pages 49, 71 & 77
© Kerstin Rodgers / Redferns / Retna Ltd., page 59
© Ken Settle, page 87
© J. Scott Wynn / Retna Ltd., page 99